PRICE FOR PEACE

Plan for the Future and Live Your Life NOW
7 Clever Knows of Getting Insured Right

Huria Kiran
Award Winning Author

10-10-10
Publishing

Publisher
10-10-10 Publishing
Markham, ON
Canada

Printed in the United States of America

Table of Contents

DEDICATION

I want to dedicate this book to my mother, Jamila Naz. The independence and trust that she gave me are the real reason for my strength and confidence.

I want to dedicate this book to my sweetheart daughter, Ishmal, who is the most precious gift of God for me.

ABOUT THE AUTHOR

Huria Kiran is Certified Life Insurance Expert, based out of Ontario. Huria works with families and business owners to develop sound financial plans. She is an expert in her field due to her dedication to the profession, her willingness to learn and adapt, and her continued education through reading and experience. She has a Master's degree in Commerce. Her mission is to educate and spread financial knowledge to help people to make informed financial decisions. Huria grew up in Pakistan and, in her 20s, ventured over to Canada as an immigrant. She is the oldest of five children.

To send Huria a message, or ask her a question, like her Facebook page, *Price for Peace*, or contact her through her website, **www.price4peace.com.**

FOREWORD

I am extremely impressed with **Huria Kiran,** who rises to the top as the "Life Insurance Expert."

Huria has chosen to share her wisdom about the industry challenges you can face in the journey of financial peace. Her book, *Price for Peace* also gives you a bird's eye view of why financial planning is important, and explains why getting it done right, and at a very affordable price, will provide you with priceless peace in your family and business life.

If you have been given this book by an advisor, understand that they want the best for you and your loved ones.

This is a must read, especially if you are starting a family. Huria can help you to look ahead, so you can take the necessary steps to avoid a financial disaster.

Raymond Aaron
New York Times Bestselling Author

Chapter 1

Price for Peace

"Live your life. Take chances. Be crazy. Don't wait, because right now is the oldest you've ever been, and the youngest you'll ever be again."

Chapter 1 – Price for Peace

- Understanding the Peace
- Purpose of a Financial Plan
- Financial Plan at the Right Price
- Ingredients of a Peaceful Financial Plan
- The Price Tag

Understanding the Peace

It is said that nothing is free in this world and, yes, there is a price for each and every thing. Sometimes that price is visible in the form of *materials,* and sometimes it is invisible, in the form of *emotions.* Let's understand the *Wheel of Life* to realize our priorities.

[1]The *Wheel of Life* is a great tool to help you improve your life balance. It helps you quickly and graphically identify the areas in your life to which you want to devote more energy, and helps you understand where you might want to cut back.That's when it's time to take a *helicopter view* of your life, so that you can bring things back into balance.

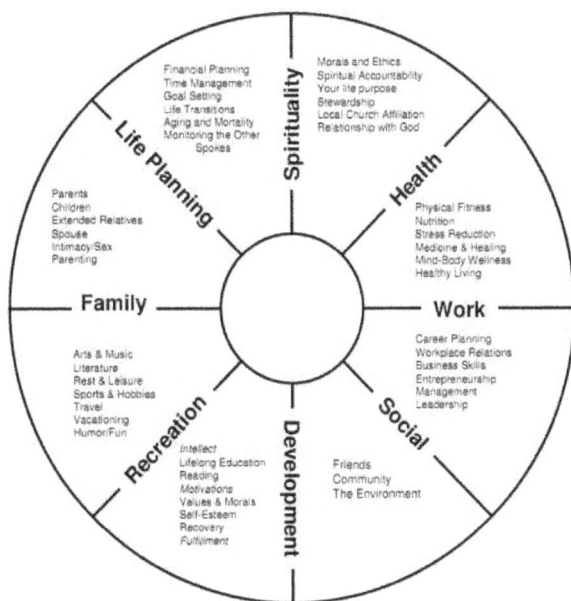

If we cannot control situations/happenings around the globe, we should not even care about them, as these are not in our control. Worrying about uncontrollable factors will simply waste our energy, time, and focus. For example, we cannot control accidents, deaths, disabilities, earthquakes, floods, storms, fires, international politics,... and the list goes on. If we can't control them, it's useless to worry about them; it's better that we focus and plan for the factors we can control, and that matter. If we take a look at the *Wheel of Life*, there are 8 segments of our life we need to keep in balance. Health has always been the most important, but it depends on how we manage our lifestyle, relationships, and finances, and how we deal with stress. (42% of Canadians are stressed due to finances.)

"Things we can control, matter, and we should focus on those."

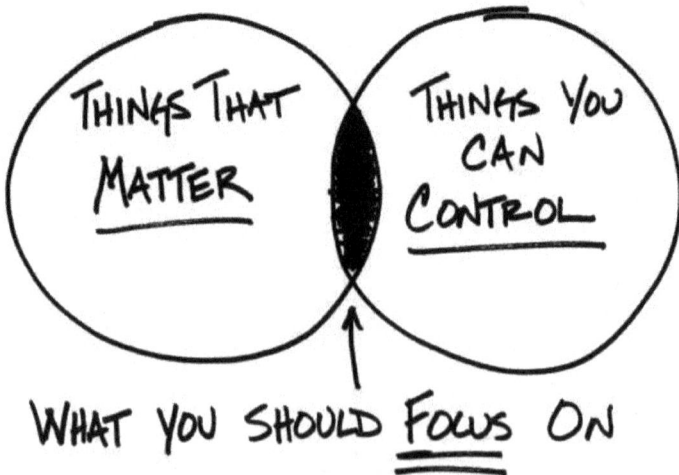

THINGS THAT MATTER

THINGS YOU CAN CONTROL

WHAT YOU SHOULD FOCUS ON

For the scope of this book, I will be discussing the financial aspect of our lives for balanced and peaceful living, whether we talk about ourselves, family, or business, as it matters the *MOST*. That's where our focus should be. We can control financial stress by having a safety net.

In our family, if someone dies or gets sick, the first shock is *emotional*: we cannot control and measure. The 2nd shock, which is controllable and measurable, is *financial*. In our lives, our whole focus should be on things we can control in order to be peaceful. If something so priceless and precious can still be had with a small price, how can you ignore it and not want to have it?

Again, for emotional shock, in the case of death or sickness of a family member, you need time to heal; on the other hand, the other shock is financial, and you have to deal with this right away.

Moreover, the answer is proper financial planning so that you can be *RICH AT YOUR POOREST TIME.*

Right Financial Plan=Price for Peace

The good price is what will make us free from financial worries: a balanced plan that will be a good match for your needs and will be within your budget.

In short, the focus should be on the *financial shock*, which we can control, somewhat. In the next chapters, I will be discussing the main ingredients, how they work, and the precautions we should take to have a peaceful life for our loved ones and ourselves.

Purpose of a Financial Plan

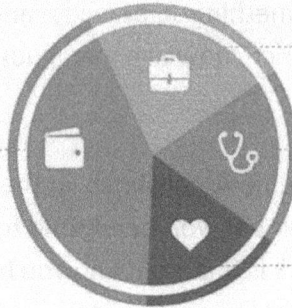

What's stressing Canadians?

42% of Canadians ranked 'money' as their greatest stress

42% Money

23% Work

19% Personal Health

17% Relationships

[2]The major purpose and reason for financial planning is to line up our financial and lifestyle ducks. Most people have a lot going on financially—RRSPs, TSFAs, life insurance, pension plans, education funds, taxes, employee benefits, wills, power of attornies, and cash flow, to mention a few—and with life in general.

DEFINITION of Personal Finance: all financial decisions and activities of an individual. This could include budgeting, insurance, savings, investing, debt servicing, mortgages, and more. Financial planning involves analyzing the current financial position and predicting short-term and long-term needs.

A financial plan looks at your current situation and future goals. It defines short and long-term financial goals and sets targets to achieve them.

[3]Some of the objectives normally targeted in the strategic financial plan include:

- Planning the retirement income
- Preparing for the purchase of a home
- Leaving a legacy
- Lowering the taxes
- Protecting assets from creditors
- Understanding the insurance coverage
- Planning for higher education
- Managing the cash flow

In conservative words, the base of the right financial plan = the right combination of insurance and savings.

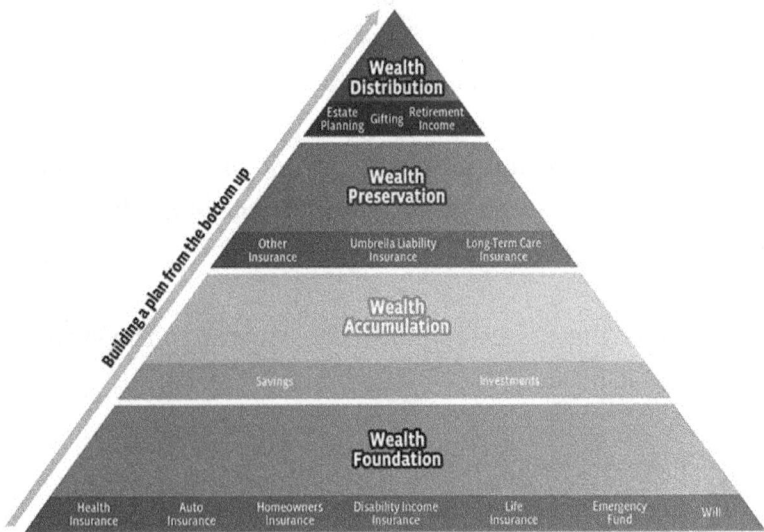

Financial Plan at the Right Price

Many Canadians think that financial planning is only about investing for retirement. It is—but it is also so much more. Whether planning for education, or graduates planning to pay off debt, or a senior planning to leave assets to the next generation, financial planning is how one should think ahead to achieve goals.

Ingredients of a Peaceful Financial Plan

Any well-designed personal financial plan should include life insurance, savings, and investments. Sometimes the lines that separate these three distinct financial products get blurred because particular types of life insurance include saving and

Allows you to reach your specific goals without having to compromise your standard of living

Helps you plan your investments, retirement, taxes, children education, children marriage, property etc.

Need for Financial Planning

Helps you asses your risk profile and develop appropriate asset allocation strategy

Provides direction and meaning to all your financial decisions leading to more discipline choices in life

investing components. When it comes to planning/budget, examine all three of these categories separately for best results.

The ensuring family is the 1st step and the foundation of the Financial plan, and the next step is to save for emergencies, education, and retirement. The 3rd step is Investing, and enjoying the growth.For the scope of this book, I will be discussing the base, as Protection is the base of the Financial pyramid.

To build a strong platform, the base has to be strong or it may fall.

"Insurance should form the bedrock of any Financial Plan."

Insurance should constitute the bedrock of any financial plan – to make sure the basics are right.

By ensuring some protection, it helps to pay out a lump sum in the event of sudden death or disability, and then a regular savings plan to create ongoing wealth.

[4]Risk management should form the basis of any financial plan, even though discussing death and disability hardly rank as a favorite activity for most people. However, failure to plan adequately for the financial consequences involved could mean unnecessary hardship for your loved ones and you.

"It is the first thing you should look at before investing—it is critical."

[5]The easiest and most cost-effective way for most people to mitigate these risks is through insurance products such as disability, life, and long-term-care insurance.

That may be common knowledge, but according to experts, discomfort with the subjects, and the complexity of insurance products, prevents many people from obtaining necessary coverage in advance of a life-changing event.

"We have a natural inclination to avoid the topic of death and disability, but they are critical."

While people know they should be planning for these events, "it should be a bigger priority than it often is." It is like flossing: everyone knows you are supposed to do it, but few people do.

People make two mistakes with life insurance. First, they put off buying it—either because it does not seem urgent if their health is good, or because it involves having a conversation most people would rather avoid. Alternatively, they let fear drive their decision when purchasing life insurance.

"Life insurance is about replacing the economic loss, not an emotional loss. So, if you view it in that cold, hard light, you just have to calculate what that loss will be and find the right insurance plan to do that job."

The Price Tag

[6]Who can put a price tag on the well-earned peace of mind you get with life insurance? People often puzzle over whether to get life insurance or not. Retirees and mature moms think critically about the costs vs. the benefits.

However, it only comes down to just an individual question: "Would my untimely passing lead to financial straits for any of my loved ones?" If you are thinking "yes," it is the right time for a life insurance policy. Life insurance gives the much-needed facet of peace of mind to your life, and you might even live longer without the stress, which would be ironic.

Adding Up Your Insurance Needs

[7]The insurance decisions should be based on family, age, and economic situation. There are many forms of insurance and,

unfortunately, not a one-size-fits-all policy. Life insurance, for example, can be a virtual necessity, if you have a spouse and children. Disability insurance, which provides an income stream in the event one is unable to work, is necessary for everyone.

Finally, if you win the lottery, you might be able to cancel your life insurance policy. If you are wealthy enough, you can insure yourself. Otherwise, you should re-evaluate your life insurance needs each time your life situation changes significantly, to make sure that anyone who would be financially affected by your death or sickness, will be taken care of.

Just for fun, someone asked me,

"Is there Relationship insurance?You know,in case someone steals your significant other? If not,there should be."

Again, it's the *emotional* side with relationships, that only time can heal; I can only help for *financial* peace—visit www.insurecanadian.com for more information.

[1] www.mindtools.com
[2] finanzafp.com/ & planfirst.ca
[3] www.strongwealthmanagement.com
[4] www.usatoday.com
[5] familylifefinancialservices.net
[6] www.lifeinsurancefinder.com.au
[7] www.axa-equitable.com

Chapter 2

Insurance VS Savings

Chapter 2 – Insurance VS Savings

- Identification
- Keep Investments and Insurance Separate
- The Financial Planning Pyramid
- Understand the Pyramid to determine priorities
- Buy Term/Invest the difference Approach

[8]Financial security means different things to different people. In his book, *Richistan*, Robert Frank interviewed people from all socioeconomic levels and found that everybody, regardless of what they made, said they would feel financially secure if they made twice as much as their current income. At a more practical level, most working families have *two choices* for financial security in emergencies: a savings plan or insurance.

Any well-designed personal financial plan should include life insurance, savings, and investments. Sometimes the lines that separate these three distinct financial products get blurred because particular types of life insurance include saving and investing components. When it comes to planning/budgeting , examine all three of these categories separately for best results.

Identification

[9]Savings is money that you set aside for emergencies or big ticket items. These funds should be kept in a safe account that is readily accessible, such as a bank savings or money market account. Investments involve risk but are also expected to produce a higher rate of return than savings. Investments may include stocks, mutual funds, and real estate. Life insurance is a policy that promises to provide a monetary settlement to help provide for loved ones in the event of your death.

[10]**Insurance** is a way of managing risks. When you buy insurance, you transfer the cost of a potential loss to the insurance company in exchange for a fee, known as

the **premium**. Insurance companies invest the funds securely, so it can grow, and pay out when there's a claim.

Savings is income *not spent*, or deferred consumption. Methods of saving include putting money aside in, for example, a deposit account, a pension account, an investment fund, or as cash.[1] Saving also involves reducing expenditures, such as recurring costs. In terms of personal finance, saving specifies low-risk preservation of money, as in a deposit account, versus investment, wherein risk is higher; in economics, more broadly, it refers to any income not used for immediate consumption.

Keep Investments and Insurance Separate

Keep your insurance and investments separate. Whole life insurance may be attractive because, once you have it, you cannot lose it if you become ill. However, whole life insurance is also expensive, so it may be difficult to afford the premiums to get the coverage you need. Whole life insurance should not be used for savings or as an investment because the return on your premiums in the form of cash value is low in comparison to other investment choices. Typically, you are better off purchasing a higher face amount of term insurance, at a much lower premium, and investing the difference in higher-yielding financial instruments.

Must-Have Insurance

[11]Before you consider going without any insurance, remember that some kinds of coverage are mandatory. If you drive, you must have auto insurance. If you buy a home with a mortgage, the lending bank will require you to carry homeowners insurance to protect its collateral. One must have life and health insurance (In a few cases, health insurance is provided by an employer.). Do not go without any of these forms of insurance, as the risks of being unprotected far outweigh the benefits of saving money in the short term.

Benefits of Savings

When you pay premiums for an insurance policy, that money belongs to the insurance company. If you never suffer a loss, you get nothing for that investment. By contrast, the money you put into a savings plan does not just remain your money; it earns interest while it sits unused in the account.

Benefits of Insurance

The advantage of insurance is instant access to the large amounts of money a disaster sometimes requires. If you put $150 a month into savings instead of buying a disability insurance policy, and you are hurt next month, you only have $150 to see you through your recovery. The disability insurance policy would give you income immediately.

Combined Approach

Many financial experts recommend a combined approach to the insurance vs. savings question. This plan means buying the insurance you need and depositing money regularly into an emergency fund. If the emergency fund grows to the point that you have enough money to do without a policy, cancel the policy. In time, you will have a savings account big enough for most disasters, and more cash flow because you have eliminated most of your premium payments.

To start a financial plan, you need to combine both main components—insurance and savings—but there are always some constraints you have to consider. The main concern is mostly affordability. A 35 year old man who has two kids, and his wife is a homemaker, needs life insurance and disability insurance; at the same time, they should save for an emergency fund, kids' education, and retirement. It may be very tough to put the right Insurance and savings plan into place, and in the budget.

So, here is a challenge—if you cannot do your best, do good; or, at least do something. Start from the base and, step-by-step, add as your financial position get better.

The Financial Planning Pyramid

Earlier this year, I took a class that focused on meeting clients' needs. Little did I know that I would end up focusing on my needs first! I am an insurance agent, but I am also a consumer.

As a consumer, I want the best overall value. To me, this means I will pay a fair price for the appropriate amount of insurance protection that I feel is necessary. I am acutely aware that the cheapest plan might not be the best plan, but if this is the route I decide to take, I am the one at risk. I am on the hook for what my insurance does not cover.

As an insurance agent, I want to give my clients and friends the options for the best protection they can, and should, have, within reason and within their budget. In my class, we reviewed *The Financial Planning Pyramid.* The instructor drilled into our brains how important the foundation is, and how if we as consumers do not have a solid foundation, the rest can very quickly become very pointless. Within the foundation, there is insurance protection—health insurance, disability income insurance, homeowners insurance, auto insurance, life insurance—but also an emergency fund and a will. All are very important protection elements; without one of these blocks of protection, it could place additional risk on the other building blocks within the pyramid.

[12]The financial planning pyramid is one of the most useful tools to make your plan, partly for its simple logic, and partly for the ease with which it can be adapted to your personal circumstances.

Understand the Pyramid to Determine Priorities

[13]A comprehensive financial plan should take everything into account to provide you with a clear picture of where you are now and where you want to be in the future. It looks at short-term and long-term financial goals to help you prepare for the kind of retirement you deserve. By following the plan you establish, and monitoring and updating it on a regular basis, your pension can be as financially secure as it is personally satisfying. Below are the elements you have to consider in developing a financial plan, in the form of a pyramid... all built on a solid base with a sound financial plan. The bottom items of the pyramid should be addressed before moving to the top of the pyramid. This ensures you have a strong base.

A financial plan can help you to:

- Protect what is most important to you
- Save money you need to realize your goals
- Plan for retirement
- Leave something for your family
- Manage your taxes

Here is the pyramid:

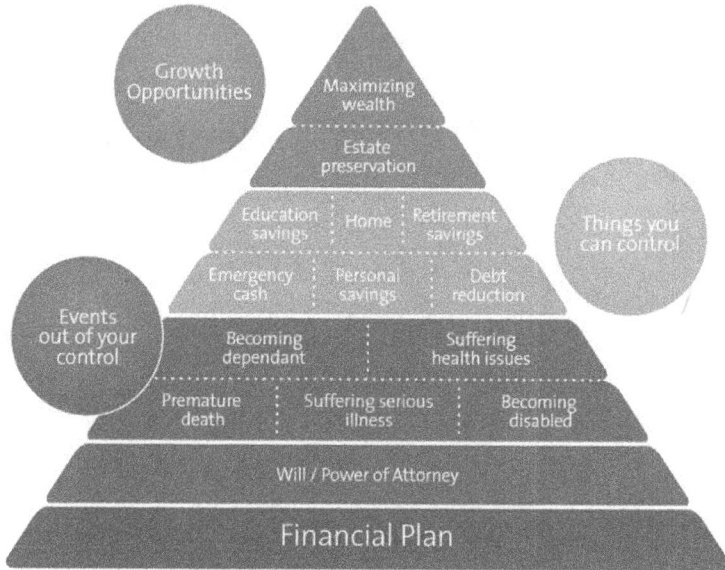

Events that you cannot control, we can cover by having proper protection. On the other hand, things you can control, we can accomplish by having a proper Savings plan.

Note: To get a will done, you need a lawyer, or it can be done online as well, with very nominal charges.

Protection is the Priority

The base is Defensive Planning, where you need to cover the risks for you and for loved ones.

What you earn + What you own + What you Owe + Those you love

Needs
Pyramid

Pass Along
Assets
· Estate Conservation
· Charitable Giving
· Consider Tax Efficiency
· Business Continuation Planning

Progressive
Planning

Potential
Financial
Success

Aggressive
Planning

Prioritize Goals
· Diversity to Reduce Risk
· Maximize Qualified Plan Contributions
· Overpower Inflation

Potential
Financial
Security

Offensive
Planning

Plan For
· Major Purchases   · College Education
· Emergencies   · Retirement

Defensive
Planning

Protect
· What You Earn   · What You Owe
· What You Own   · Those You Love

For educational purposes only.

Buy Term/Invest the Difference Approach

[14]When you buy a term policy, all of your premiums go toward securing a death benefit for your beneficiaries, who are usually your spouse or children. Term life insurance, unlike permanent life insurance, does not have any cash value and, therefore, does not have any investment component. However, you can think of term life insurance as an investment in the

sense that you are paying relatively little in premiums in exchange for a relatively large death benefit.

For example, a nonsmoking, 30-year-old woman, in excellent health, might be able to get a 20-year term policy with a death benefit of $1 million for $480 per year. If this lady dies at age 49 after paying premiums for 19 years, her beneficiaries will receive $1 million tax-free—and she paid in just $9,120. Term life insurance provides an incomparable return on investment should your beneficiaries ever have to use it. That being said, it provides a negative return on investment if you are in the majority of policyholders whose beneficiaries never file a claim. In that case, you will have paid a relatively low price for peace of mind, and you can celebrate the fact that you're still alive.

Do you hate the idea of potentially *throwing away* almost $10,000 over the next 20 years? What would happen if you invested $480 per year in the stock market instead? If you earned an average annual return of 8%, you'd have $25,960 after 20 years, before taxes and inflation. Considering the opportunity cost of putting that $480 per year into term life insurance premiums instead of investing it, you're really *throwing away* $25,960. However, if you die without life insurance during those 20 years, you'll leave your heirs with almost nothing, instead of leaving them with $1 million.

What if you bought permanent life insurance instead? The same woman described above, who purchased a whole life insurance policy from the same insurance company, could expect to pay $9,370 annually.The entire life policy's cost for a *single* year is just slightly less than the term life policy's cost for *20* years. So, how much cash value are you building up for that extra cost?

- After five years, the policy's guaranteed cash value is $19,880, and you will have paid $46,850 in premiums.

- After ten years, the policy's guaranteed cash value is $65,630, and you will have paid $93,700 in premiums.

– After 20 years, the policy's guaranteed cash value is $181,630, and you will have paid $187,400 in premiums.

However, after 20 years, if you had bought term for $480 a year and invested the $8,890 difference, you'd have $480,806 before taxes and inflation, at an average annual return of 8%.

"Sure," you say, but the permanent life insurance policy *guarantees* that return. I'm not guaranteed an 8% return in the market. That is true. If you have no tolerance for risk, you can put the extra $8,890 a year in a savings account. You'll earn 1% annually, assuming interest rates never go up from today's historic lows. After 20 years, you'll have $208,671. That is still more than the permanent policy's guaranteed cash value of $181,630.

Finally, using permanent life insurance as an investment might make sense for some people in some situations (usually high-net-worth individuals looking for a way to minimize estate taxes).

For the average person, the odds are poor that permanent life insurance will be a good investment compared with buying term, and investing the difference.

Visit www.insurecanadian.com for more information.

[8] www.finance.zacks.com
[9] en.wikipedia.org
[10] www.balarinsuranceadviser.com
[11] www.finance.zacks.com
[12] www.financialplanninginfoguide.com
[13] www.thesteelgroup.ca
[14] www.insurancealexparker.blogspot.com

Chapter 3

Life Insurance: Putting a Price on Peace of Mind

Chapter 3 – Life Insurance: Putting A Price On Peace Of Mind

"Peace of Mind, Otherwise Known as Life Insurance."

- Why do we need Insurance?
- Life Insurance = Death + Living Benefits
- Who Needs and Qualifies for Life Insurance?
- Understanding Life Insurance
- How Insurance Benefits Individual
- How Insurance Benefits Business
- Non-medical life insurance
- Traditional Life Insurance Products
- Difference between Term and Permanent Life Insurance
- Common Living Benefits of Disability insurance.

"Peace of Mind, Otherwise Known as Life Insurance. It's an Act of Love."

Protecting family with life insurance is a caring and responsible act. With this simple step, one can ensure their loved ones a secure future.

[15]Life insurance cannot replace a loved one, but it will replace the income that you may have depended on, and it can help keep family intact. Life insurance benefits can help with all sorts of living expenses, from covering a house mortgage to paying school tuition.

Why Do We Need Insurance?

Why LIFE INSURANCE?

1. What keeps your family from having to change the lifestyle you provided?
2. What can ensure your assets are passed on to the next generation?
3. What helps keep a business stable at the death of a partner or owner?

Don't let sudden tragedy uproot your family or bankrupt your business. Even after you pass, there are still people who rely on you.

Insurance is a way of managing risks. When buying insurance, one transfers the cost of a potential loss to the insurance company in exchange for a fee, known as the **premium**. Insurance companies invest the funds securely, so it can grow, and pay out when there's a claim.

"You Never Know." None of us can predict the future, but having life insurance can protect you from whatever may happen in your own personal *Crystal Ball of Life*. It is like having a safety net.

[16]If you are wondering whether or not one should buy life insurance, ask yourself this one question: "Would my death leave anyone in a financial bind?" If you answer "yes," it may be time to get serious about shopping for life insurance. Life insurance can offer peace of mind, ensuring that your debts or loved ones will be taken care of in the event of your death. However, before you buy it, you need to ask yourself if you will qualify, and whether you should purchase term or permanent life insurance.

Life Insurance = Death + Living Benefits

*If a child, a spouse, a life partner, or a parent
depends on you and your income, you need life insurance.*
Suze Orman
QuotesHDWallpapers.com

Who Needs Life Insurance?

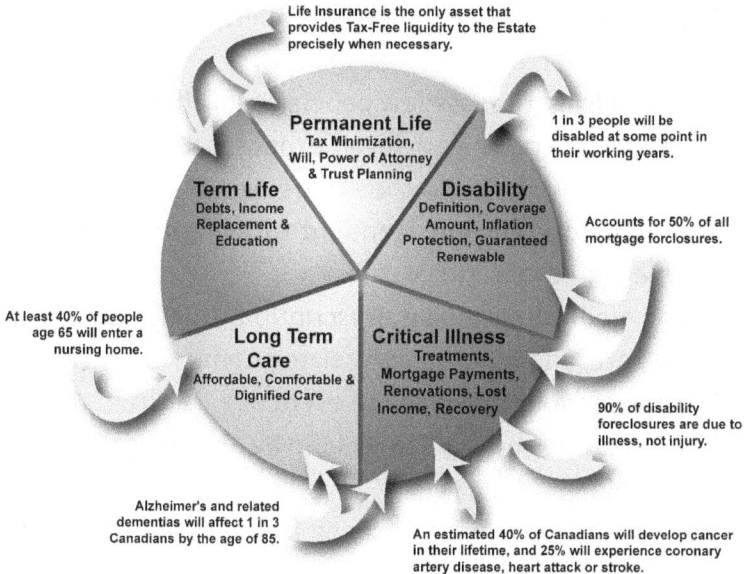

Life Insurance is the only asset that provides Tax-Free liquidity to the Estate precisely when necessary.

Permanent Life
Tax Minimization, Will, Power of Attorney & Trust Planning

1 in 3 people will be disabled at some point in their working years.

Term Life
Debts, Income Replacement & Education

Disability
Definition, Coverage Amount, Inflation Protection, Guaranteed Renewable

Accounts for 50% of all mortgage forclosures.

At least 40% of people age 65 will enter a nursing home.

Long Term Care
Affordable, Comfortable & Dignified Care

Critical Illness
Treatments, Mortgage Payments, Renovations, Lost Income, Recovery

90% of disability foreclosures are due to illness, not injury.

Alzheimer's and related dementias will affect 1 in 3 Canadians by the age of 85.

An estimated 40% of Canadians will develop cancer in their lifetime, and 25% will experience coronary artery disease, heart attack or stroke.

[17]The rule of thumb is once you become a parent, any adult in your house earning income should have life insurance coverage that will last until your youngest child completes college. If you have significant financial obligations such as high credit-card debt or a mortgage, you could use life insurance to ensure that debt is covered. Because life-insurance death benefits are exempt from federal taxation, many financial planners often use clients' life-insurance benefits to help pay for the estate taxes generated by the passing of a loved one.

Insurance helps you:

- **Own a home**, because mortgage lenders need to know your home is protected
- **Drive vehicles**, because few people could afford the repairs, health care costs, and legal expenses associated with collisions and injuries, without coverage
- **Maintain your current standard of living** if you become disabled or have a critical illness
- **Cover medical costs** like prescription drugs, dental care, vision care, and other health-related items
- **Provide for your family** in the event of a death
- **Run a** small business or family farm by managing the risks of ownership
- **Take** vacations without worrying about flight cancellations or other potential issues

[18]You have worked hard to build a solid financial footing for you and your family, so you want to be sure that everything is protected. Accidents and disasters can and do happen; if you are not adequately insured, it could leave you in financial ruin. You need insurance to protect your life, your ability to earn income, and to keep a roof over your head.

Who Needs and Qualifies for Life Insurance?

"Excuses will always be there for you, opportunity won't."

[19]To determine if you qualify, most life-insurance policies require you to undergo a medical exam, primarily to check for high cholesterol and blood-sugar levels. Before issuing a policy, the insurance company will also check things such as your medical history, hobbies, credit rating, alcohol-related issues, and driving record, just to name a few. Factors such as age, smoking, and prior health issues can also drive up the premiums on a policy.

Understanding Life Insurance

The Role of Insurance in Your Financial Planning

[20]When used effectively as part of an overall financial or estate plan, life insurance and other types of insurance products can serve many purposes for both individuals and businesses.

How Insurance Benefits Individuals

Below are some of the most important reasons why you should consider insurance in your financial/estate plan:

Estate Preservation

You can offset the costs that are incurred at death and preserve your estate by having the insurance proceeds pay them for you. Taxes, liabilities, estate-related and other future costs can all be offset by your permanent coverage.

Tax Minimization

Tax-exempt insurance (such as universal or whole life insurance) can eliminate the annual taxes you pay on your investment growth, as well as those payable when you die. Individuals tired of being punished for strong earnings may appreciate such an opportunity.

Estate Maximization

By taking advantage of the tax-preferred status of universal or whole life insurance, you can maximize the value of assets you plan to pass on to the next generation. The long-term value of these products can often far eclipse what would otherwise be earned through regular investing.

Wealth Creation

If you are in the early stages of wealth accumulation, insurance can be a low-cost way to create a financial safety net in the event there is a loss of an income earner.

Income Enhancement

Certain insurance products can provide a supplemental stream of income during retirement. The net income derived from this strategy may be significantly higher than what is achievable with traditional fixed-income vehicles, especially during times of low-interest rates.

Liquidity

When the unexpected occurs, insurance proceeds can provide much-needed funds to cover financial obligations like taxes, outstanding bills, and last-minute expenses. These proceeds are allowed to bypass the estate and, therefore, the entire probate process. That means these funds will not be held up in court or subject to fees that normally apply to the rest of your estates, such as executor, lawyer, and accounting fees.

Disability Protection

Most people understand the benefit of life insurance as financial protection against death, but few realize that the odds are far greater that a person will become disabled. This would mean a major loss of income for your family. You might also consider how long your investment portfolio would last if you were forced to liquidate to replace that income. Disability insurance can provide funds to offset living expenses during times of sickness or accident.

Charitable Giving

Several insurance products and strategies allow you to provide funds to charities of your choice, in the most cost and tax-effective way possible.

Diversification

We all have the same pools of capital within which to invest. However, life insurance is another pool of capital—a tax-exempt one that can add another layer of diversification to your overall asset allocation strategy. It is an excellent way to complement the rest of your overall portfolio; by moving a small percentage of your non-registered pool into a policy each year, you can further diversify your interests and spread your assets over one more pool of capital, namely your tax-exempt life insurance pool.

How Insurance Benefits Business

Below are some of the top insurance strategies you may wish to consider as a business owner:

Funding Buyout Agreements

In the case of partnerships, the death or disability of one partner can have a devastating effect on the survival of business. Insurance can provide an excellent method of funding buyout agreements so that the remaining partner takes full control of the business and the surviving family is properly compensated.

Shared Ownership

For companies who wish to retain top employees, the shared ownership of a permanent insurance policy can be an attractive opportunity. It protects the company against the death of the employee and motivates that person to remain with the firm through the enticement of an attractive, low-cost retirement asset.

Minimize Corporate Taxes

If corporate assets are invested in fixed income, then an insurance strategy can not only reduce its taxable income, but it will lower the value of the business by the amount of the investment, thereby reducing the inevitable capital gains tax liability.

Maximize Corporate Assets

By taking advantage of tax-deferred growth inside universal or whole life insurance, corporate assets can avoid accrual taxation and grow to a much greater value than if they were invested in a regular account. Not only that but, upon death, most, if not all, of the proceeds can be paid out of the corporation, tax-free. Ordinarily, they would be paid out as taxable dividends, requiring approximately 1/3 of the value to be paid in taxes.

Traditional Life Insurance Products

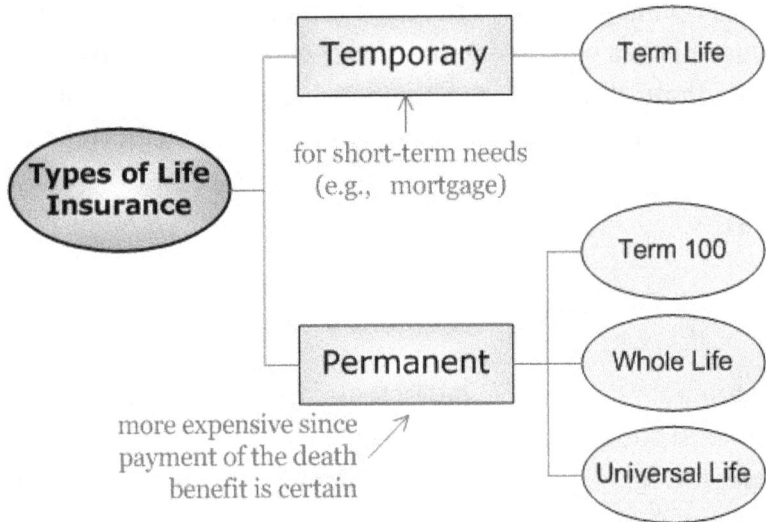

Types of Life Insurance

Temporary — Term Life

for short-term needs (e.g., mortgage)

Permanent — Term 100 / Whole Life / Universal Life

more expensive since payment of the death benefit is certain

Permanent and Temporary Insurance

First, you need to understand the two basic types of life insurance: term and permanent.

Term life insurance provides a predetermined death benefit and covers you for a predetermined number of years, usually five to 30. The annual premiums are fixed and are based on your health and life expectancy at the time you apply for the policy.

Permanent life insurance combines a death benefit with a savings or investment account. The policy covers you for as long as you are alive, even if you live to be 100. The premiums can be fixed or not, depending on the policy your purchase. Like term life insurance, the premiums are based on your health and medical history.

Permanent life insurance is not the best choice for most people. It is several times as expensive as term life insurance for the same amount of coverage. While your policy does accumulate some cash value through its savings or investment component, which a term policy does not have, you pay a hefty premium for this feature and for having a policy that will pay out one day. A term policy will hopefully expire before you do.

An oft-touted benefit of the permanent policy's cash account is that you can borrow against it. However, with the money, you could save by purchasing term insurance . Instead, you could amass your nest egg so that you do not need to borrow anything to pay for a large expense. Also, when you borrow against your permanent life insurance policy, you diminish the policy's value and can defeat the purpose of even having life insurance.

Difference Between Term & Permanent Life Insurance

[21]The difference between term and permanent life insurance is quite simple. Term life insurance pays a predetermined sum if the insured dies during a given period. For that reason, it can usually be obtained at an affordable rate.

On the other hand, permanent life insurance provides lifetime protection that does not expire. Most permanent policies offer a savings or investment component combined with the insurance coverage. For that reason, the premiums for permanent insurance are more costly than term policies.

Term Life Insurance

[22]Term life insurance is pure insurance protection that pays a predetermined sum if the insured dies during a specified period. On the death of the insured, term insurance pays the face value of the policy to the named beneficiary. All premiums paid are used to cover the cost of insurance protection.

The term may be one, five, 10, or 20 years or longer. However, unless renewed, the insurance coverage ends when the term of the policy expires. Since this is temporary insurance coverage, it is the least expensive to acquire. A healthy 35-year-old (non-smoker) can typically obtain a 20-year level premium policy with a $250,000 face value, for between $20-$30 per month. Here are the key features of term life insurance:

* Temporary insurance protection
* Low cost
* No cash value
* Usually renewable
* Sometimes convertible to permanent life insurance

Permanent Life Insurance

Permanent life insurance provides lifetime insurance protection (does not expire), but the premiums must be paid on time. Most permanent policies offer a savings or investment component combined with the insurance coverage. This component, in turn, causes premiums to be higher than those of term insurance. The investment may offer a fixed interest rate or may be in the form of money market securities, bonds, or mutual funds. This savings portion of the policy allows the policy owner to build a cash value within the policy which can be borrowed or distributed at some time in the future.

Here are the key features of permanent life insurance:

- Permanent insurance protection
- More expensive to own
- Builds cash value
- Loans are permitted against the policy
- Favorable tax treatment of policy earnings
- Level premiums

There are three basic types of permanent insurance: whole life, variable life, and universal life. The two most common are whole life and universal life. Whole life insurance provides lifetime protection, for which you pay a predetermined premium. Cash values usually have a minimum guaranteed rate of interest, and the death benefit is a fixed amount. Whole life insurance is the most expensive life-insurance product available.

Universal life insurance separates the investment and the death benefit portions. The investment choices available usually include some equity investments, which may make your cash value accumulate quicker, as you can usually change your premiums and death benefits to suit your current budget.

[23]Policies often have a deferred payout, meaning that the life insurance amount is limited to a return-of-premium plus interest, in the first two policy years, when the death has not been ruled an accident. Understand the contract before committing.

Also, when seeking insurance, don't rush into buying expensive, permanent life insurance before considering if term life insurance sufficiently meets your needs. Unfortunately, in many cases, the fees charged for policies with investment features far outweigh the benefits. When you purchase life insurance, you are betting that you will live, but also securing peace of mind in case you are wrong. Don't leave your family unprotected in the sudden event of your death—after all, they are your most valuable assets.

To have a peaceful financial plan, we need the RIGHT mix of the below as per our need and budget.

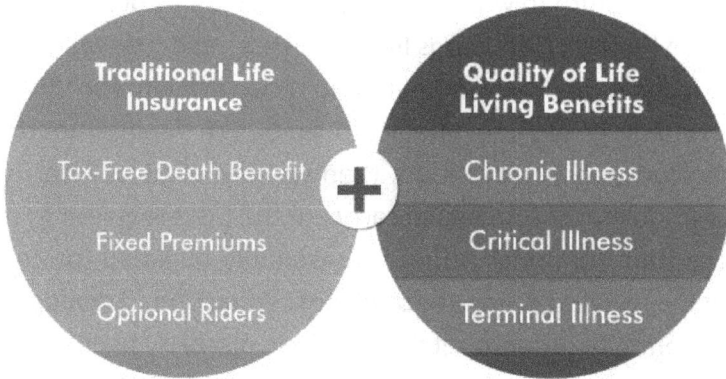

Traditional Life Insurance	Quality of Life Living Benefits
Tax-Free Death Benefit	Chronic Illness
Fixed Premiums	Critical Illness
Optional Riders	Terminal Illness

Common Living Benefits of Disability Insurance

Let's learn more about how disability insurance can help protect you and your family from an unexpected illness or accident which leaves you unable to earn an income:

What types of disability insurance are there?

[24]**Short Term Disability Insurance** provides temporary income replacement if you are unable to work due to a medical condition (injury or illness). Usually, this policy only covers income replacement for the first 120 days. Short term disability insurance benefits are purchased by employers for their employees.

Long Term Disability Insurance offers a form of income protection if an illness or disability leaves you wholly or entirely unable to return to work. It provides you with a portion of your income that can go towards living expenses and that which may also include medical treatment and rehabilitation. For the first two years, if you are unable to meet the requirements of performing your occupation, then you are eligible. After two years, you must be unable to carry out the tasks required by any occupation for which you are reasonably qualified, or could become qualified for, because of education, training, or experience, in order to retain long-term disability benefits.

Critical Illness Insurance provides financial support if a person is diagnosed with a *critical* illness. Depending on the policy you purchase, it may include cancer, stroke, heart disease, heart attack and, usually, 10–20 other serious medical conditions. These benefits will be paid regardless of the person's ability to return to work. The benefit is paid in one lump sum; however, there is a *survival period* for typically 30 days once diagnosed with the condition which must pass before that person can receive benefits.

Disability Mortgage Insurance provides you with financial support if you become disabled and are unable to work. This policy covers all or part of your mortgage payment up to a certain amount, bi-weekly or per month. There is typically a 60-day waiting period before you can receive benefits. There are also limitations in regards to duration and the amount of coverage that will be given.

Long-Term Care Insurance Long-term care is not just for seniors. According to the Canadian Life and Health Insurance Association, one in three people will be disabled for 90 days or more at least once before they reach age 65. Long-term care insurance can cover some of the costs of a care facility, such as a long-term care, convalescent or nursing home, following an accident or as a result of illness. Many long-term care plans also cover the services of a caregiver in your home.

To qualify for benefits, most plans state that you must be incapable of performing two or more activities of daily living by yourself, such as bathing, dressing, or feeding.

While many long-term care facilities receive government funding, most also charge co-payments or extra fees for additional services.

There is also public funding for home-care services, but you may have to make co-payments or need additional services that are not provided under the long-term plan. You may want to consider buying insurance to cover these costs.

You will typically have to wait 30 to 90 days after becoming incapacitated before you begin to receive benefits. Some additional conditions and restrictions may apply.

For more information, see the Canadian Life and Health Insurance Association's Guide to long-term care insurance.

Finally,

"Buying life insurance is like fixing a leak in your roof.
The longer you wait ,the more expensive it gets."

On the other hand, one of every two foreclosures is due to a disability; only 2 % are due to death. What we need is the right mix of life and living benefits.

Visit www.insurecanadian.com *for more information.*

[15] www.jrcinsurancegroup.com
[16] www.knowledgefinancial.com
[17] www.investopedia.com
[18] www.ibrokers.co.nz/resource.html
[19] www.investopedia.com
[20] www.rbcds.com
[21] www.investopedia.com
[22] www.moneysavvy.blogspot.com
[23] www.tools.insureye.com
[24] www.injurylawyercanada.com

Chapter 4

Life Insurance 101

LIFE INSURANCE

**"LIFE INSURANCE IS THE ONLY TOOL THAT TAKES PENNIES
AND GUARANTEES DOLLARS."**
-Ben Foldman

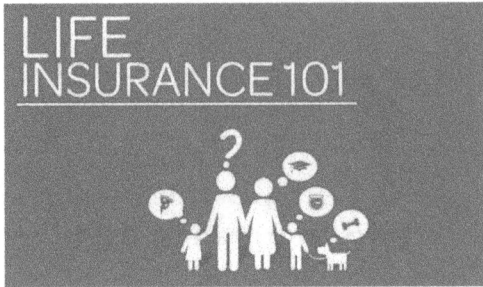

Chapter 4 – Life Insurance 101

- How Does It Work?
- Who Should Obtain Term Life Insurance?
- Types of Term Insurance
- Term Life Insurance Quotes
- How Quotes Are Determined
- Why Quotes Vary
- Importance of Life Insurance Company Ratings
- Permanent Life Insurance 101
- Whole Life Insurance 101
- Universal Life Insurance 101
- Is Life Insurance A Smart Investment?

It is very critical to understand different death benefits available in the market, and how they work, so that you can make a conscious decision with having sufficient knowledge.Only then can you pay the right price for peace when you perform due diligence.

[25]Life insurance is also a valuable estate planning and tax saving tool. Life insurance debts are exempt from federal taxation. A financial professional may advise one to use life insurance benefits to help pay for estate taxes accumulated upon the death of a loved one. Whether you have no life insurance, or you have not reviewed your policy in a while, it is always a good idea to be aware of your options and be prepared.

Let's start with term insurance, which is cheapest, and suitable in most of the cases.

Term Life Insurance 101

Term life insurance is a vital way to protect your loved ones financially after you die. Obtaining it offers peace of mind. It also guarantees your debts will be covered and your loved ones will be provided for.

.

Term insurance is arguably the least expensive and easiest type of life insurance you can purchase. It provides basic protection against your death. Your beneficiary receives a lump sum in an amount of your choosing in such an event. This type of insurance is also temporary. It provides coverage for just a designated period. The typical time span is during your working years.

If you are unsure of how much to designate for life insurance, consider using your mortgage balance as a base amount. If a couple relies more on one spouse's income, think about making the higher-income spouse's policy even larger than the necessary mortgage amount, so the lower-income spouse has something left over after the mortgage is paid.

Starting a family? Consider adding additional term life insurance. Some financial experts suggest adding ten times your annual income if you have kids under ten years old, and five times your annual income if you have kids over 10. If you cannot afford that much coverage, just do what you can. Less coverage always beats zero coverage.

How Does It Work?

As previously stated, term life insurance is in place for a period designated by you. The most common terms are 10, 20, and 30-year periods. The insurance policy continues to be valid for as long as you pay the premium. One of the benefits of term life insurance is the fact that the premium amount will never increase, regardless of the condition of your health.

A typical term life insurance coverage policy also guarantees a designated dying benefit. You set this specific amount, and it will never change, regardless of the length of the policy. It means that the insurance provider will pay that exact amount to your beneficiaries whether you die on the first day of coverage or the last.

Who Should Obtain Term Life Insurance?

Term life insurance is an excellent choice for those looking to provide income replacement for their families should something happen to them. More specifically, this type of insurance provides solid, affordable protection for those that have children, carry significant financial obligations, or own a company. (For more, see: Using Indexed Universal Life for Retirement Income.)

Types of Term Insurance

Level Term: This is the most commonly purchased type of term insurance. The term *level* refers to the death benefit amount during the duration of the policy; so, it pays the same benefit amount if death occurs at any point during the term. Common types of the level term are:

- Yearly renewable term
- 5-year renewable term
- 10-year term
- 15-year term
- 20-year term
- 25-year term
- 30-year term
- Term to a specified age (usually 65)

Decreasing Term: Unlike level term, the death benefit in this type of insurance decreases at a predetermined rate over the life of the policy. Premiums are usually constant throughout the contract, and reductions in policy payout usually occur monthly or annually. Term lengths can vary from between one and 30 years.

The main benefit of decreasing term policies is their affordability. The theory behind them is that a person's insurance coverage needs decrease with age and when certain liabilities and debts no longer exist. Decreasing term insurance is not advisable for someone with no other life insurance.

Term Life Insurance Quotes

Life insurance rates are mainly based on your health. If you are in good health, then it is easier to obtain a cheaper policy. However, if you have a high-risk health condition, then the price of your coverage could be much higher. Different companies make different assessments based on a person's medical background and how risky they believe you are to insure.

The process of obtaining a quote from a company includes going through a medical exam, after which a company will compare their results to your medical records. You will then receive a quote from the business that reflects your risk class, the amount of coverage you are seeking, and the level of term insurance you desire.

Remember, a quote is not the same as an actual offer. For instance, your health may not be at the same level you thought it was. An increase in price could stem from high cholesterol, high blood pressure, or other findings in your medical records you did not disclose in your initial phone interview with the insurance company.

If your premiums are much too high due to medical reasons or you are denied coverage, check if a group plan is available through your business. These group plans do not require a medical exam or a physical.

How Quotes Are Determined

To break it down further, let's closely examine some of the specific factors an insurance carrier's underwriters will look at when determining a policy's premium quote.

Age – Your age can make a major difference in the premium quote that you receive. Because of the health risks that come with age, prices for insurance increase significantly over time. Applying for term life insurance while you are still young is ideal, as it is an affordable way to obtain a significant amount of coverage.

"Fun is like life Insurance—the older you get, the more it costs."

Gender – This is also a significant factor in the premium price of life insurance. Since research shows that women tend to live several years longer than men, females will usually pay a lower premium.

Height and Weight – These measurements are important to insurance companies. Since obesity is considered to be a high-risk factor in life insurance coverage, premiums may be significantly higher for those deemed to be overweight.

Smoking Status – Smoking is regarded as one of the highest risks to life expectancy and is one of the biggest factors in premium rates for all types of life insurance coverage. Those who are smokers or use other forms of tobacco can pay a staggering *five times more* than non-smokers.

Health Status – Most life insurance companies require that applicants complete a medical exam to determine his or her overall health status. This usually includes blood pressure and heart rate readings, as well as blood and urine samples.

Lifestyle – Life insurance applicants are also typically interviewed about lifestyle choices. A company then determines if they are considered risky or dangerous habits. Activities that could result in higher premium rates for the applicant could include skydiving, hang gliding, scuba diving, or race car driving.

The level of Coverage – Understandably, the higher the amount of coverage you wish to purchase, the more expensive your life insurance premium will be.

Why Quotes Vary

The premium quote a person is offered for the same life insurance policy can widely vary depending on the company. While some criteria for evaluating applicants can be similar, certain factors can differ from company to company. For example, some companies now take an applicant's driving record into account when evaluating their level of risk, while others do not. (For more, see: When to Update Your Life Insurance Beneficiaries.)

For this reason, it is important to compare quotes from various companies before making a final decision on where you will obtain coverage. One way to accomplish this in an easy manner is to work with either a business or agency that has access to multiple insurance carriers. Then you can quickly compare policies, carriers, benefits, and premium rates, and choose the policy that makes the most sense for your situation. The goal is to find an insurer that will provide you with the best protection for the most affordable price. You can research the financial soundness of your insurer at A.M. Best.

Importance of Life Insurance Company Ratings

When shopping for the most affordable life insurance, it is important to factor an insurance company's rating into your final decision. Find out whether a particular business is financially stable and has an excellent reputation for paying out its policyholder claims. Obtaining cheap life insurance is not worth it if the company is not reputable.

Some of the businesses that provide insurance ratings include Standard & Poor's, M. Best, Fitch, Moody's, Dun & Bradstreet, and Egan-Jones Rating Company. These companies typically give insurance companies ratings in the form of a letter grade, with A++ being the highest.

The Better Business Bureau (BBB) is another good source that reveals how well an insurer pays its claims and the quality of its customer service. This organization will provide a letter grade. It also gives details regarding any complaints that have been filed with the company.

Difference Between Term and Permanent Life Insurance

The difference between term and permanent life insurance is quite simple. Term life insurance pays a predetermined sum if the insured dies during a given period. For that reason, it can usually be obtained at an affordable rate.

On the other hand, permanent life insurance provides lifetime protection that does not expire. Most permanent policies offer a savings or investment component combined with the insurance coverage. For that reason, the premiums for permanent insurance are more costly than term policies.

Tip

Term life insurance is an affordable way to obtain protection for your loved ones after your death. Hopefully, you now realize it is important not to rush into purchasing a policy. Take time to consider whether a particular policy meets your needs for the price, and seek advice from professionals.

Permanent Life Insurance 101

[26]"What's in a name?" When it comes to buying life insurance, everything is in the name. Permanent life insurance is one such example of a name you will hear when you are in the process of buying life insurance. However, what does it mean?

Before settling on a specific life insurance policy, you must analyze your family's needs, both pre-death and post-death. There are two main types of permanent life insurance:

Whole life insurance – Caters to long-term goals by offering consumers consistent premiums and guaranteed cash value accumulation.

Universal life insurance – Gives consumers flexibility in the premium payments, death benefits, and the savings element of their policy.

Permanent Life Policy

This type of life insurance provides lifetime coverage. It is typically comprised of two parts: savings or investment portion, and an insurance portion.

Due to the presence of the savings element, the premiums are quite high. Here, a part of your premium (after deducting the insurance expenses) is invested by your insurance company, and the accrued interest builds up your cash value. For this reason, permanent life insurance is also known as cash value insurance.

The most important feature of a permanent life policy is that you can take a policy loan by borrowing against your cash value. Note that in a permanent life policy, the face value amount is different from the cash value. Face value is the amount of insurance you have bought and that your beneficiaries will receive upon your death. Cash value is the accumulated savings that you can access in the future.

To be able to borrow against the policy, you need to have a good amount of cash value as you cannot borrow against the policy's face value. This option is quite favorable because the interest rates offered by the insurers are comparatively lower than prevailing market rates. If you default, the insurance company will use the cash value to cover the amount borrowed. The best thing is that you can get this policy loan without any restrictions on how to use it and without any of the hassles involved with credit checks.

Occasionally, your unexpected financial expenses do not allow you to pay the premiums on time. If you do not have enough cash value, then non-payment of premiums can result in cancellation of your policy, or it may be converted into a reduced paid-up policy. Due to the strict guidelines of a permanent policy, the only safeguard here is the use of the stored cash value in the policy to cover the premium payment. You can use your cash value for premium payment to continue your insurance coverage. Here, also, you need to make sure that your cash value has accumulated an ample amount of money.

In case you want to cancel your permanent life policy, you will get your cash value in hand and can use it at the time of emergency. You need to bear in mind, however, that permanent life insurance policies are specially made to be kept in force for the lifetime of the insured. It may be foolish to surrender your policy after five years, so be sure to consult your insurance advisor before taking this step.

Whole Life Insurance 101

Whole life insurance covers you as long as you live. You have to pay the same amount of premium for a given period to receive the death benefit. Normally, this policy is kept in force for the rest of your life, regardless of how long you may live. This type of insurance provides life insurance coverage with a savings feature. As a result, you may end up paying higher premiums in the beginning compared to term life insurance.

Here, your insurance company puts part of your insurance money in a high-interest bank account. With every premium payment, your cash value increases. This savings element of your policy builds up your cash value on a tax-deferred basis. In a way, the presence of guaranteed cash values makes this policy worthwhile because you can borrow against your cash value or surrender your policy to get the cash value in hard cash.

You can also opt to participate in the surplus of your insurance company and receive the dividends annually. Here again, you have the choice to either get your dividends in cash or let them accumulate interest. You may also use your dividends to reduce your policy's premiums or buy additional coverage. Consult your insurance advisor before the purchase of a whole life policy from a particular insurance company because dividends are not always guaranteed.

Whole life insurance is made to fulfill an individual's long-term goals, and it is important that you keep it in force for as long as you live. It is advisable to buy whole life insurance when you are younger so that you can afford to pay for it in the long term. Unlike term insurance, the level premiums, fixed death benefits, and the attractive living benefits (like loans and dividends), make this policy quite expensive.

In conclusion, you practically pay premiums throughout your lifetime, and take advantage of the cash value benefits while you are alive, and upon death, since your nominees get the death benefits. Whole life insurance is highly suitable for long term responsibilities like your surviving spouse's income needs and post-death expenses.

Universal Life Insurance 101

This policy is also termed *adjustable life insurance,* because it offers more flexibility compared to whole life insurance. You have the liberty to reduce or increase your death benefit and also to pay your premiums at any time and in any amount (subject to certain limits) after your first premium payment has been made.

Here, you can increase the face value of your insurance coverage. However, you need to pass a medical examination to qualify for this benefit. Similarly, you may decrease your coverage to a minimum amount without surrendering your policy. However, surrender charges may be applied against the cash value of your policy.

When it comes to the death benefit, you have two options: a fixed amount of death benefit or an increasing death benefit equal to the face value of your policy, plus your cash value amount.

You also have the opportunity to change the amount and frequency of premium payments. So, you can increase your premiums or may also even pay a lump sum according to the specified limit in the policy. As you know, part of your premium, minus the cost of insurance, is put into an investment account, and the interest, therein, is credited to your account. In this way, the interest grows on a tax-deferred basis, which increases your cash value.

In the case of a financial hitch, you can reduce or stop your premiums and use your cash value to pay premiums. Nevertheless, there should be enough money accumulated in your cash value account to cover the premium payments. Make sure to discuss the status of your cash value fund with your insurance advisor before stopping the premiums. Your policy may lapse only if you have ceased to pay premiums and have insufficient cash value to cover the cost of insurance.

The alternative of policy loan is an added perk in universal life insurance. It is significant that you do not make repeated withdrawals from your accumulated fund. This reduces the cash value amount and will render you helpless at the time of genuine need.

Another good thing about universal life insurance is that your insurance company discloses the entire cost of insurance to you. This gives you an idea of how your policy works.

The downside of universal life insurance is the interest rate. If the policy performs well, there are chances of potential growth in a savings fund. On the other hand, the bad performance of your policy means the estimated returns are not earned. Hence, you end up paying higher premiums to get your cash value account going. Second, surrender charges may be levied at the time of terminating your policy or withdrawing money from the account.

Universal life insurance offers all-round protection to your loved ones, thanks to its security, flexibility, and variety of investment options. In times of low liquidity, you can alter your premium payments or may even withdraw from your cash value fund. Also, you can increase or decrease the face value of your insurance as per your circumstances.

Finally, when buying a particular life insurance policy, top priority must be given to your family's pressing needs. Permanent life insurance is designed to give you and your family lifelong security. Whole life insurance protects your beneficiaries in your absence and acts as an asset-accumulating tool, while universal life insurance gives you the chance to regulate your insurance coverage in keeping with your current condition. Of course, your insurance advisor is always there to help you pick a policy but, in the end, it is you who has to decide what is suitable for you and your loved ones.

	Term Insurance	Term 100 Insurance	Whole Life Insurance	Universal Life Insurance
Coverage	For a specified term	For life	For life	For Life
Premiums	Guaranteed (usually remain level for each term and then increase for the next term)	Guaranteed (usually remain level)	Guaranteed (usually remain level)	Flexible Premiums that can be increased/decreased by policy holder
Death Benefit	Guaranteed	Guaranteed	Guaranteed	Guaranteed (accumulated cash value may be added)
Cash Value Component	None	Usually none	Guaranteed	Flexible cash values depending on investment returns and level of premium deposits
Dividends	None	None	Payable on participating policies	None

Comparison Chart

Is Life Insurance a Smart Investment?

[27]When it comes to considering life insurance as an investment, you have probably heard the adage, "Buy term, and invest the difference." This advice is based on the idea that term life insurance is the best choice for most individuals because it is the least expensive type of life insurance and leaves money free for other investments. Permanent life insurance, the other major category of life insurance, allows policyholders to accumulate cash value, while term does not, but there are exorbitant management fees and agent commissions associated

with permanent policies, and many financial advisers consider these charges a waste of money.

When you hear financial consultants and, more often, life insurance agents advocating for life insurance as an investment, they are referring to the cash-value component of permanent life insurance and the ways you can invest and borrow this money. When does it make sense to invest in life insurance in this way, and when are you better off buying term and investing the difference? Let's take a look at some of the most popular arguments for investing in permanent life insurance and how other investment possibilities compare.

Arguments for Using Permanent Life Insurance As an Investment

[28]There are many arguments for using permanent life insurance. The issue is: These benefits are not unique to permanent life insurance. You often can get them in other ways without paying the high management expenses and agent commissions that come with permanent life insurance. Let's examine a few of the most widely advocated benefits of permanent life insurance, one by one.

1. You get tax-deferred growth.

This benefit of the cash-value component of a permanent life insurance policy means you do not pay taxes on any interest, dividends, or capital gains in your life insurance policy until you withdraw the proceeds. You can get this same benefit, however, by putting your money in an RRSP or a TFSA.

If you are maxing out your contributions to these accounts year after year, permanent life insurance might have a place in your portfolio.

2. You can keep your policy until age 100, as long as you pay the premiums.

[29]A key advertised benefit of permanent life insurance over term life insurance is that you do not lose your coverage after a set number of years. A term policy ends when you reach the end of your term, which for many policyholders is at age 65 or 70. However, by the time you are 100, who will need your death benefit? Most likely, the people you originally took out a life insurance policy to protect—your spouse and children—are either self-sufficient or have also passed away.

3. You can borrow against the cash value to buy a house or send your kids to college, without paying taxes or penalties.

You can also use the money you put in a savings account that you control—one on which you do not pay fees and commissions—to buy a house or send your kids to college. However, what insurance agents mean when they make this point is that if you put money in a tax-advantaged retirement plan and want to take it out for a purpose other than retirement, you might have to pay a 10% early distribution penalty, plus the income tax that's due. Furthermore, some retirement plans make it difficult or even impossible to take out money for one of these purposes.

That being said, it is generally a bad idea to jeopardize your retirement by raiding your retirement savings for some other purpose, penalties or not. It is also a bad idea to confuse life insurance with a savings account. What's more, when you borrow money from your permanent insurance policy, it will accrue interest until you repay it and, if you die before repaying the loan, your heirs will receive a smaller death benefit.

4. Permanent life insurance can provide accelerated benefits if you become critically or terminally ill.

You may be able to receive anywhere from 25% to 100% of your permanent life insurance policy's death benefit before you die if you develop a specified condition such as heart attack, stroke, invasive cancer, or end-stage renal failure. The upside of accelerated benefits, as they're called, is that you can use them to pay your medical bills and possibly enjoy a better quality of life in your final months. The drawback is that your beneficiaries will not receive the full benefit you intended when you took out the policy. Also, your health insurance might already provide sufficient coverage for your medical bills.

Also, some term policies offer this feature; it is not unique to permanent life insurance. Some policies charge extra for accelerated benefits, too—as if permanent life insurance premiums were not already high enough. **Finally, understand the plans available, and how they work, before making a**

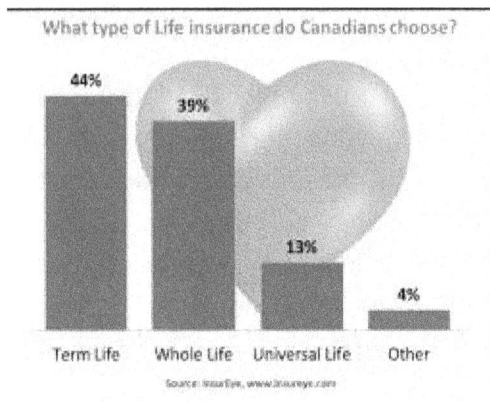

What type of Life insurance do Canadians choose?

44% Term Life
39% Whole Life
13% Universal Life
4% Other

Source: InsurEye, www.insureye.com

purchase. In most cases, **Term Life Insurance is simply what you need, as this chart shows:**

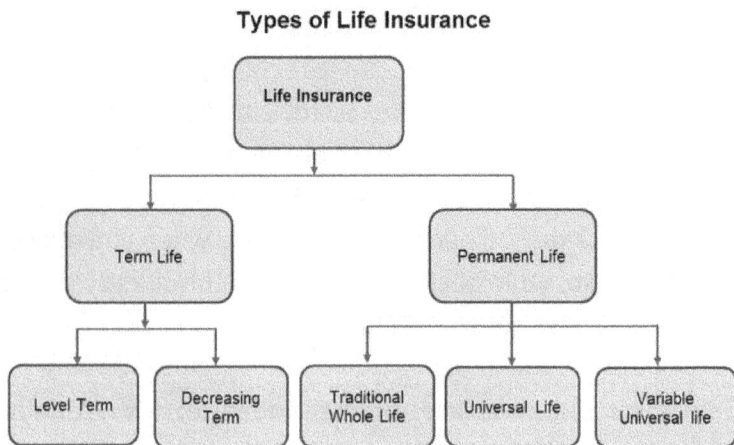

Types of Life Insurance

Life Insurance

Term Life — Permanent Life

Level Term | Decreasing Term | Traditional Whole Life | Universal Life | Variable Universal life

Market Realist

Source: Metlife, Various Sources

Finally:

Term Insurance = Pure Death Benefit

Whole Life Insurance = Death Benefit + Cash Values

Universal life insurance = Death Benefit + Cash Value + Investment Features

Visit www.insurecanadian.com for more information.

[25] www.investopedia.com
[26] www.lifeofxen.com
[27] www.affordableinsgrp.com
[28] www.insurancealexparker.blogspot.com
[29] www.affordableinsgrp.com

Chapter 5

Living Benefits of Life Insurance

Chapter 5 – Living Benefits of Life Insurance

"Saving your life shouldn't cost your life savings."
- Introduction
- Disability Insurance
- Disability Insurance Features
- Critical Illness
- Critical Illness Features
- Long Term Care
- Long Term Care Features
- 5 K's of Long Term Care
- Health and Care
- 7 K's of Health Insurance
- Travel Insurance
- 9 K's of Buying Travel Insurance
- Using Cash Value for Living Benefit

"Medical bills are the leading cause of bankruptcy, and these bills can be avoided by having medical insurance."

Introduction

[30]The irony of life **insurance** is that the **benefit** is realized at the death of the policyholder. It is real **death insurance,** but that would be a hard idea to sell. **Living benefit** plans are **insurance** policies that provide financial **benefits** to survivors who face issues due to aging, illness, accidents, and dependency.

Life insurance policies are no longer being utilized only when one passes away. Today, policy benefits can be more *customized* for other needs as well—and this is helping consumers to use their plans for some unique needs and goals.

There are five common types of living benefit insurance policies:

- Disability Insurance
- Critical Illness
- Heath and Dental
- Long Term Care
- Travel Insurance

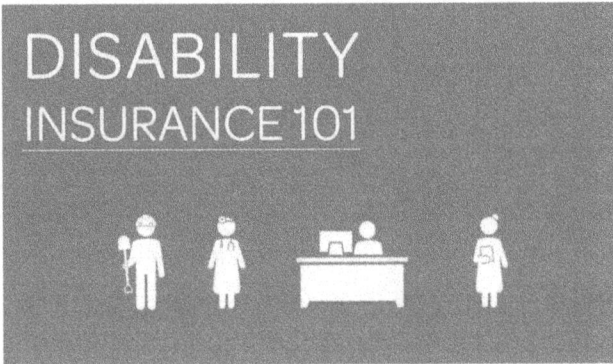

DISABILITY
INSURANCE 101

"People buy insurance not because they will die but because their incomes will."

31

Your greatest asset is your paycheck. Disability Insurance protects you and your family if you are unable to work, by providing income that will help pay your bills and take care of your family. It's just as important as life Insurance.

A recent study conducted by an insurance company showed:

Probability of Incurring a 90-Day or Longer Total Disability

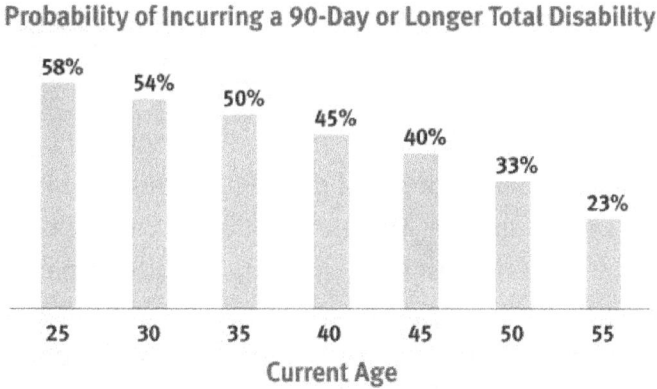

[32]Disability insurance (sometimes called DI) is an insurance policy that pays out a stream of monthly income in case you get disabled and cannot work. The injury or disability does not have to have happened at work, but it must be severe enough to prevent you from working and earning an income. Many people have both short term disability and long term disability coverage through work, but you can buy personal disability policies if there is no coverage, like in the case of some self-employed individuals, or if you are not covered after working hours.

Understanding the Product

[33]There are three main definitions of disability when looking at a disability insurance contract:

• Any Occupation

Under this definition, total disability means the inability to work at any occupation. Therefore, if the insured is a computer consultant, and the disability prevents them from performing his or her regular occupation duties, but they can still work as a checkout clerk, the insured would not receive any money.

• Regular Occupation

Under this definition, total disability means the inability to work at the insured's regular occupation due to an injury or illness.

• Own occupation

This is the gold standard definition of disability. Under this definition, total disability is also defined as the inability to work at your regular occupation, regardless of whether you work in another gainful occupation.

Many variables go into designing a disability policy, and each one of them impacts pricing:

• **The monthly indemnity**

The amount the insured would receive.

• **The elimination period**

How long until the insured begins to receive their disability benefit.

• **The benefit period**

How long they receive their money for.

Available Riders

There is a whole host of riders that can be added to disability policies, including a cost of living benefit, which increases the monthly indemnity by adding a cost of living allowance. A future income option is also available. This allows the insured to upgrade their coverage in the future, based on their revenues and not on medical criteria. Other riders, such as return-of-premium options, which can return all or part of the premium depending on the company and the policy, are an option as well.

RBC Insurance

CANADIANS OFF WORK DUE TO A DISABILITY FACE A PERFECT STORM

43% Canadian working households have had someone take time off work due to disability

1 in 3 Canadians will experience a period of disability lasting longer than 90 days during their working lives[1]

BEING OFF WORK TAKES A FINANCIAL & EMOTIONAL TOLL

48% Canadians not financially prepared to be off work

78% Canadians said finances were tight when off work

81% Canadians upset about not being able to work

STRESS ON THE FAMILY

76% said it was stressful for the entire household

50% said family relationships were strained

31% said their able partner had to find extra work to make ends meet

EMPTYING THE PIGGYBANK

29% dipped into savings to pay for expenses
17% borrowed money from family and friends
17% took on more debt
9% cashed in RRSPs

TIPS TO HELP WORKERS OFF WITH A DISABILITY

- Investigate how your workplace benefits define a disability, and what is and isn't covered. Ask about employee assistance programs.
- Be proactive and formulate a "return to work plan" with your employer and family.
- Ask your medical professionals about services or programs that are available to make sure you're getting the care you need to recover.
- Explore your 'Return to Work Benefits' such as financial planning, job search and retraining, rehabilitation and other services to help make a smooth transition back into the workplace.

® / ™ Trademark(s) of Royal Bank of Canada. Used under licence.

RBC Insurance commissioned Ipsos to conduct a survey to gauge public opinion of Canadian workers regarding matters related to disability, financial preparedness around disability and attitudes towards disability. The survey was conducted between June 10 to 16, 2015. In total, a sample of employed working Canadians was surveyed online using Ipsos' I-Say online panel. The selection of specific online surveys are measured using a credibility interval. In this case the results are considered accurate to within ± 3.0 percentage points, 19 times out of 20, had the entire population of Canadian workers been polled. ¹Commissioners disability table A.

Critical Illness Insurance

"If you get sick, the last thing you should have to worry about is Finance."

[34]Critical illness insurance provides a lump sum payment when a specific condition is diagnosed. The money can then be used for any purpose. Some examples include finding alternative medical treatments anywhere in the world, hiring a caregiver, paying debts, covering expenses that are not covered under government health care, paying for private nursing homes, or providing income support. Many different conditions might be covered under a critical illness policy, but the most common are heart attacks, strokes, and cancer.

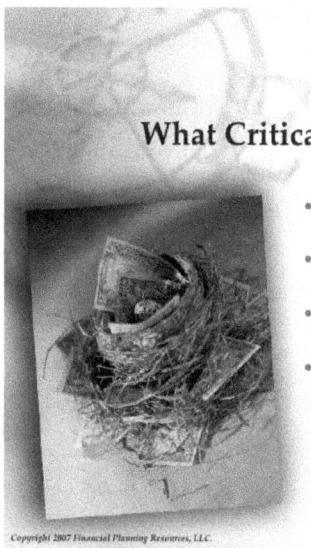

Critical Illness Insurance

What Critical Illness Insurance Does

- Immediate pay-out upon confirmed diagnosis of a covered condition
- Absolutely no restriction on how funds used
- No impact on other benefits, such as health insurance, Medicare, etc.
- *Benefits are income-tax free.*

Copyright 2007 Financial Planning Resources, LLC

Critical Illness Features

[35]Critical illness policies are generally much more aggressively underwritten than life insurance policies. Critical illness underwriting looks more deeply into family health history than life insurance applications.Critical illness insurance is not tied to the insured's income or his or her ability to go back to work. The coverage pays out a lump sum regardless of the insured's revenue or his or her ability to remain employed. Instead, the benefit is strictly tied to the definition of the critical illness diagnosis according to the insurance company.There are no occupation classifications for critical illness, unlike disability insurance, which provides better classifications for select occupations and thus, lower premiums. Critical illness just looks at the insured's gender, age, smoking status, and overall health when determining the premiums.

Common causes of *critical illness claims*: Cancer 64%; Heart Attack 11%; Stroke 8%; Coronory Artery Bypass Surgery 3%; Other 14%.

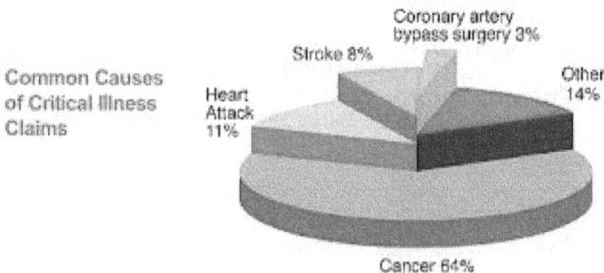

Common Causes of Critical Illness Claims

Coronary artery bypass surgery 3%
Stroke 8%
Heart Attack 11%
Other 14%
Cancer 64%

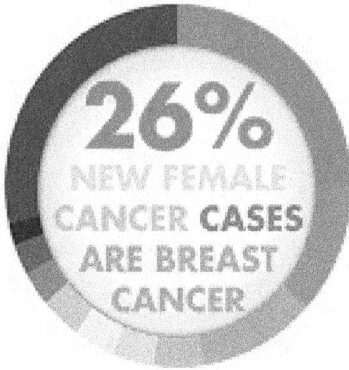

- 26% Breast Cancer
- 12% Lung Cancer
- 11% Bowel Cancer
- 5% Uterus Cancer
- 4% Ovarian Cancer
- 4% Non-Hodgkin Lymphoma
- 4% Malignant Melanoma
- 3% Brain Cancer
- 3% Pancreatic Cancer
- 2% Kidney Cancer
- 29% Other Cancers

Health and Dental Coverage

[36]Like disability insurance, health and dental plans are often covered through workplace benefits. These plans are designed to help with the unexpected cost of healthcare needs when you need it. There is a growing concern that governments will have significant cutbacks in the health care industry and, as a result, the financial burden of prescription drugs, visits to the dentist, eye exams, and paramedical services may increase in the future. Individual Health and Dental Insurance policies can be purchased through insurance companies, as well as provincial Blue Cross organizations.

7 K's of Health Insurance

- Premium
- Deductables
- Copay
- Exclusions
- Lifetime Maximum
- Out of Pocket
- Coordination of Benefits

Important Terms To Know About Health Insurance

PREMIUM
A premium is an amount we pay to the health insurance company each month to preserve our coverage. The premium is the first thing to consider when tries understanding the cost of a health insurance plan.

DEDUCTIBLES
The amount we owe for health care services our health insurance covers before our health insurance or plan begins to pay. For example, if the deductible is $1,000, the plan won't pay anything until you have met your $1,000 deductible for covered health care services subject to the deductible.

CO-PAY
Copayment or co pay is a payment defined in the insurance policy and paid by the insured person every time when a medical service is accessed. It is a form of coinsurance, but is defined differently in the health insurance where a coinsurance is a percentage payment after the deductible up to a certain limit. It must be paid before any policy benefit is payable by an insurance company.

EXCLUSIONS
A health insurance exclusion refers to anything the insurance company will not cover. These exclusions can vary from plan to plan, and it's essential that you get to know your plan's exclusions.

LIFE TIME MAXIMUM
The lifetime maximum insurance benefit is the maximum amount that your insurance company will pay during your lifetime. The range of lifetime maximum benefit limits can vary widely.

OUT OF POCKET
The most you pay during a policy period (usually one year) before your health insurance or plan starts to pay 100% for covered essential health benefits. This limit must include deductibles, coinsurance, copayments, or similar charges and any other expenditure.

COORDINATION OF BENEFIT
Coordination of Benefits (COB) is the process of determining which of two or more insurance policies will have the primary responsibility of processing/paying a claim and the extent to which the other policies will contribute.

Issued in public interest by BFC CARE

BFC Care

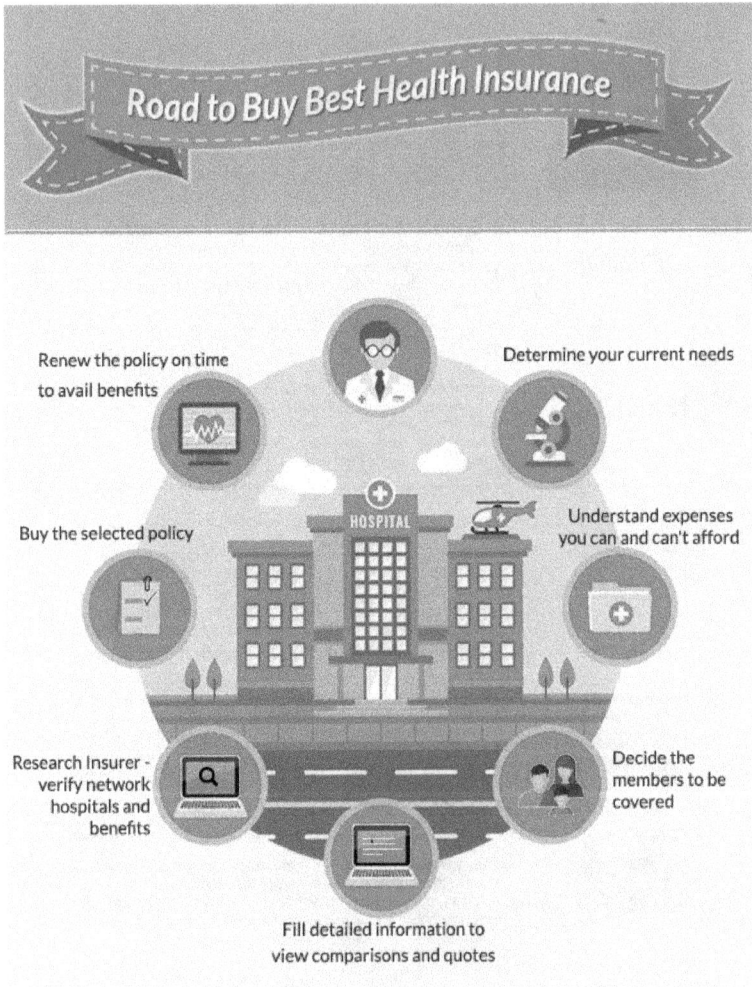

Road to Buy Best Health Insurance

Renew the policy on time to avail benefits

Determine your current needs

Buy the selected policy

HOSPITAL

Understand expenses you can and can't afford

Research Insurer - verify network hospitals and benefits

Decide the members to be covered

Fill detailed information to view comparisons and quotes

Long-Term Care Insurance

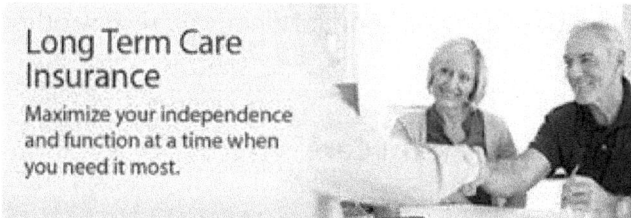

Long Term Care Insurance
Maximize your independence and function at a time when you need it most.

[37]Long-term care insurance is another coverage that is rapidly growing in popularity. This product does not just protect your wealth; it allows you to maintain your independence and dignity by taking control of your future care plans and protecting your family members from being forced to be your primary caregiver.

This plan pays a daily or monthly benefit for medical or custodial care received in a nursing facility, in a hospital, or at home if you are unable to carry out some of the common activities of daily living (ADLs). Some examples include:

- Bathing
- Dressing and undressing
- Eating
- Transferring from bed to chair, and back
- Voluntarily controlling urinary and fecal discharge
- Using the toilet
- Walking (not bedridden)

Getting insurance of any kind is a form of risk management . . . preparing for unfortunate circumstances in life. Be sure to include a review of living benefits when you review other types of insurance.

Features of Long-Term Care

LTC is the care you need when you can no longer perform daily tasks such as:
- transferring
- continence
- dressing
- toileting
- bathing
- eating

Unlike life insurance, most long-term care plans do not offer a discount to non-smokers.The plans price smokers and non-smokers at the same rate.Some carriers even price males and females at the same rate. The latter provides a good value for men but a poor value for women, because the average female lives longer and is more likely to be on a claim for a longer period The greatest threat to depleting your wealth in your retirement years is your health. Long-term care insurance provides funds to pay for ongoing costs associated with your care. Only a handful of insurance companies offer long-term care insurance in Canada, and these plan features are not standardized.

Therefore, it is a difficult product for brokers to deal with, so not many do. If you are looking to buy long-term care, your best bet is to work with a broker who specializes in long-term care insurance.

Living Benefits as Riders

Living benefits, also referred to as accelerated death benefits, can be added as a rider to life insurance policies, either at the time of purchase or afterward. These advantages will allow terminally ill individuals to access a portion of their life insurance death benefit proceeds before their death. They can be bought as a separate policy or can be added as a rider while buying life insurance, or you can buy 3-in-one or 2-in-1 policies, which will serve as life insurance and living benefits.

5 K's of Long-Term Care Insurance

- Know the elimination period and benefit period that best suits your needs and budget.
- Know the policy limitations on when and how you receive your benefits.
- Know if there's a premium cap on the policy.
- Determine if you need any riders, such as a cost of living adjustment or a return-of-premium rider.
- Know the reimbursement process.

1. Know the elimination period and benefit period that best suits your needs and budget.

[38]The elimination period refers to the amount of time that must pass before you begin to receive your weekly benefit, and the benefit period refers to how long you will receive that coverage for. Those two variables, combined with your daily benefit, will help determine your monthly premium.

2. Know the policy limitations on when and how you receive your benefits.

Many long-term care policies will pay out only if you require facility care assistance.

3. Know if there's a premium cap on the policy.

Most long-term care policies in Canada offer guaranteed premiums for only the first five policy years.

4. Determine if you need any riders, such as a cost of living adjustment or a return-of-premium rider.

The former allows your benefit to increase in line with inflation, whereas the latter returns the premium to your beneficiary in the event you pass away.

5. Know the reimbursement process

Long-term care plans usually pay on a receipt basis. As in, they reimburse the insured for expenses incurred while requiring assistance.

[39]Few companies allow the insured to spend the proceeds however they wish. This can be of value if the insured wants a family member, or someone other than a qualified healthcare professional, looking after them.

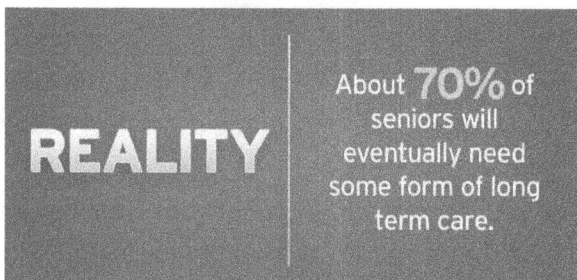

REALITY | About **70%** of seniors will eventually need some form of long term care.

Travel Insurance

[40]Travel insurance is something you can buy when you travel outside of Canada in case you get sick or have an accident while you are away. Travel insurance can cover the cost of your medical emergencies. Travel insurance may or may not include trip cancellation coverage. Most travel agencies will offer travel insurance coverage. However, you can also choose to purchase from a third party. If you are planning your trip online, or on your own, you will have to research which insurance companies are best for your needs.

When traveling outside of Canada, a trip to the emergency room or even a visit to a doctor's office can be very expensive.

Whether you are planning a month-long trek in Nepal or simply crossing the border to go outlet shopping in Buffalo or Bellingham, having coverage under a travel insurance policy is an essential part of every trip.

No one books a vacation assuming the worst, but it is something that we all have to take into serious consideration. When you are traveling, even a minor accident can quickly turn into a major expense.

Buying travel insurance and understanding what you are covered for will provide you with peace of mind, as well as a stress-free vacation.

Buying the right kind of travel insurance for your trip can be the trickiest part of planning a holiday. The subject of travel insurance has been back in the news recently in a big way, all because of one Saskatchewan family's million dollar U.S. hospital bill. Jennifer Huculak-Kimmel traveled to Hawaii while 24 weeks pregnant. She thought she had the proper travel insurance before leaving Canada but, when she delivered her baby premature and spent weeks in a U.S. hospital, Huculak-Kimmel was shocked to learn her insurance company, Blue Cross, wouldn't be helping her out with the $950,000 bill. While the reasons behind Blue Cross denying the claim have not been revealed, the company did say in a statement: "There are more facts related to this story that prevents us from reversing our decision."

It is no wonder a 2013 BMO Insurance study found that just half of Canadians purchase travel insurance before going on vacation. Whether we are shying away from insurance out of confusion over the coverage, or we think we already have insurance or just don't think insurance is all that important, the world of travel insurance can be very tricky to navigate.

So, what should you look for and know before buying travel insurance? We turned to experts from Travelzoo Canada and the Travel Health Insurance Association of Canada for the top five tips.

9 K's of Buying Travel Insurance

- Know what you are already covered for and if it is enough.
- Know if you have family coverage.
- Know if you need a multi-trip insurance policy.
- Know if you are covered or not for pre-existing conditions.
- Know that medical travel insurance and trip cancellation insurance are not the same things.
- Know that even if you are traveling within Canada, you may need travel insurance.
- Know your market.
- Know your travel insurance product. Ask many questions.
- Know the difference between Travel Agents and Insurance Specialists.

1. Know what you are already covered for and if it is enough.

[41]Many people have travel insurance through their work insurance plans or credit cards. Before you travel relying on this insurance alone, though, know what it covers, and purchase additional coverage if necessary.

Many people will already have some coverage through employers or credit cards, but it is important to understand existing coverage, and ensure you have the necessary supplemental coverage.

Some policies require you to purchase additional insurance for adventure travel, which can include hiking, bungee jumping, skiing, or even safer activities such as caving or boat tours.

2. Know if you have family coverage.

[42]Even if you already have travel insurance under an employee benefits plan, it is a good idea to *check your coverage*—out-of-country medical coverage might not be available, or may not cover your spouse or dependents.

3. Know if you need a multi-trip insurance policy.

Consider buying a **multi-trip insurance policy**, which means you will be covered for all of your trips for one annual rate. This can be a huge money saver, even if you take just a few trips each year.

4. Know if you are covered or not for pre-existing conditions.

The Travel Health Insurance Association of Canada recommends Canadians are aware of their medical history and consult with a health care provider before they fill out any insurance forms. They said the top reasons for denied claims are medical non-disclosure and misrepresentation about pre-existing conditions that are not stable.

"Responding accurately to medical forms is the best way to have a carefree holiday and ensure that unexpected medical expenses will be covered by insurance," said THIA President Alex Bittner in a statement. "If there is a medical questionnaire, it needs to be taken seriously."

[43]"I would encourage you to search for specialist travel insurers. Select insurance companies that cover people if their medical conditions are under control and stable for a given period. As a caveat, be advised that a minor change in someone's prescription or medication can mean that the medical condition is not considered *stable*.

Simply, disclose any pre-existing medical conditions you might have, and make sure to get everything in writing.

5. Know that medical travel insurance and trip cancellation insurance are not the same things.

Trip cancellation and travel health insurance are two distinct services. Trip cancellation covers pre-paid and non-refundable expenses if your plans are interrupted or canceled. The five top types of insurance are sold in a combo of sorts. If you only want one, then ask for it, and ask whether there are incentives to upgrade to all or just some. A comprehensive package covers trip cancellation and interruption, evacuation, medical, baggage, and even flight insurance.

6. Know that even if you are traveling within Canada, you may need travel insurance.

You may think your provincial health insurance will cover any medical costs across Canada, but that is not the case.

"If you plan to travel outside of your home province, it is strongly recommended that you obtain additional private medical insurance and fully understand what your policy covers," said Duchesne. "This comes into play with things like trip cancellation or interruption insurance, which covers pre-paid, non-refundable expenses should your travel plans be interrupted or canceled."

7. Know your market.

Take the time to do your research: **check out and compare rates** from your financial institution, travel insurance companies, and brokers, as well as the online travel agency you are booking with.It is always a good idea to have a Travel Insurance Specialist who can guide you to the best plan available as per your preferences, representing multiple companies.

8. Know your travel insurance product. Ask many questions:

How do you know if your medical condition is compliant with your insurance coverage? What level of coverage is right for your trip? "Direct your questions to the insurance provider directly," said Duchesne.

9. Know the difference between Travel Agents and Insurance Specialists.

Keep in mind that travel agents recommend that you get travel insurance because they get a percentage when you buy it, and because they could be held liable for losses if insurance options are not explained correctly. While they can give you information and provide direction, they are not insurance agents. It is critical to direct specific questions to the insurance provider.

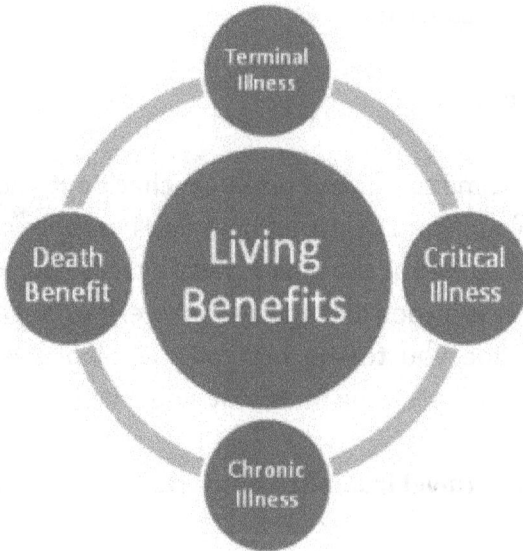

Using Cash Value for Living Benefits

The benefits from the policy can typically be accessed through either a policy surrender or a policy loan. In essence, living benefits act as a type of lien against the life insurance policy. They will reduce the death benefit that is payable to beneficiaries and can also reduce the amount that is available for loans, as well as the cash value of the policy. The lien equals the sum of the living benefits payment that the policyholder receives, plus accrued interest. However, it is always better to keep death benefits, living advantages, and savings, separate.

In short, today, with the rising cost of health care, many individuals are faced with financial hardship during an already difficult time in their lives. As one deals with both physical and emotional difficulty, the financial help, which funds from a policy's living benefits can provide, can be a welcome relief. These funds can not only relieve the stress on the individual but also on loved ones as well. Both life and living benefits are equally important, and it's important to understand the life stage you are at in order to update your plan's mix of benefits.

A study shows 48% of foreclosures are due to a CRITICAL ILLNESS.

"Saving your life shouldn't cost your life savings."

Visit www.insurecanadian.com for more information.

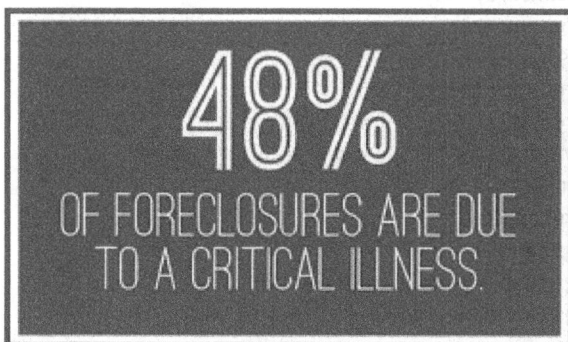

90%

of disabilities
are due to illnesses
not accidents.

Source: Council for Disability
Awareness, Long-Term Disability
Claim Review, 2014

[30] www.retirehappy.ca
[31] www.utahlifeinsurance.com
[32] www.five-ways.com
[33] www.tools.insureye.com
[34] www.retirehappy.ca
[35] www.tools.insureye.com
[36] www.retirehappy.ca
[37] www.retirehappy.ca, www.tools.insureye.com
[38] www.howtodothings.com, www.tools.insureye.com
[39] www.lsminsurance.ca
[40] www.retirehappy.ca
[41] www.blogs.canoe.ca, www.canadianliving.com
[42] www.blogs.canoe.ca, www.canadianliving.com
[43] www.blogs.canoe.ca, www.canadianliving.com

Chapter 6

Choosing the RIGHT Insurance Products

Chapter 6 – Choosing the RIGHT Insurance Products

Insurance:
- ☑ Life
- ☑ Health
- ☑ Home
- ☑ Car

A – *Must-Have* Insurance Policies

B – Must *Not Have* Policies

C – Mistakes and Solutions While Getting Insured

Before understanding types of plans, it is important to understand types of policies available and the ones you need.

There may be 2 REASONS you do *not* need a certain policy.

- The policy does not match your needs.
- You have that coverage as a sub-component of the policy you already own.

A – Must-Have Insurance Policies

[44]You can find an insurance policy to cover almost anything imaginable, but only a handful of policies are ones that you *need* to have. You work hard throughout your life to build wealth and live a happy and comfortable life, so some types of insurance can protect your possessions and income, and even provide for a loved one when you are gone.

Life Insurance

This kind of policy is more important if you are married and have children. Your life is valuable because it is what allows you to work and earn an income to provide for your family. When you are gone, you create an income gap that could put your spouse or children in financial trouble.

Death is hard enough; don't make it even harder by putting your loved ones in a financial jam if the unfortunate does happen. Funerals alone can be expensive, and it creates even more stress on the family. At the very least, you should have enough to cover basic funeral expenses and provide a cushion for your family; at most, it should provide a stream of income for your family that can replace what is now gone.

If you do not currently have life insurance, your best bet is to check with your employer first. Many employers offer a basic life insurance as a benefit, and some even allow you to purchase additional coverage at a very affordable rate. Outside of employer plans, hundreds of insurance companies can provide the right coverage for you.

Health Insurance

One of the most important types of insurance to have is health insurance.

Your good health is what allows you to work, earn money and, otherwise, enjoy life. If you were to come down with a sickness or have an accident without health insurance, you might find yourself unable to receive treatment, or even in debt to the hospital.

Thankfully, many employers provide health insurance benefits to full-time employees, and even some part-time employees. If you do not currently have health insurance coverage, this is the first place to check, as it will be the most affordable. If you are married, you may both be able to receive coverage under just one of the employer plans.

If your employer does not offer health insurance, or you are self-employed, you still need it. While it may not be cheap, the fact remains: what do you have if you do not have your health? Even a basic hospital bill, without insurance, can run into the thousands of dollars. It is not worth risking financial ruin to save a few bucks on a health insurance premium.

Property Insurance

[45]One type of policy, that for most people is mandatory to have when you have a mortgage, is homeowners insurance. If you borrow money from the bank to purchase a home, they will require the asset to be insured.

For many people, this insurance premium is built into the mortgage payment. For many people, their home is their greatest asset, so it is vital to protect it adequately.

If you rent instead of own, a renters insurance policy is just as important. Your belongings inside the dwelling can add up to a significant amount of money. In the event of a burglary, fire, or disaster, you should be able to at least have a policy that can cover most of the replacement costs.

Auto Insurance

Another type of policy that is often required is auto insurance. Most states require by law that you have basic auto insurance. While it may be a law, too many people still drive around without it.

The most common reason to have auto insurance is to cover the replacement of an expensive asset. Like a home, automobiles can be quite expensive and, if it gets damaged, you want to be able to repair or replace it. However, there is more to auto insurance than just covering the car itself.

Most automotive insurance policies cover bodily injury or death of another person in an incident that you are legally responsible for. While it pays for medical expenses related to the incident, it can also cover legal defense costs. You will also generally find medical payment coverage that pays for medical treatment for you and your passengers during an accident, regardless of who was at fault.

B – Must *Not Have* Policies

Three Insurance Policies That You Do Not Need

[46]While there are certainly more than a few types of insurance policies that have their place in people's portfolios, there are just as many that you are probably better off without. Some of these policies may sound like a good idea but, in reality, all you are doing is likely wasting money on the premiums. The following insurance types are those that most people simply don't need:

1- Mortgage Life Insurance

This kind of insurance is receiving more media coverage lately, but it is probably a policy you can do without.

Mortgage Life Insurance is a policy that promises to pay your mortgage payment in the event you become disabled or die. If you are married, this sounds like a pretty good idea, right?

Well, not exactly. This type of policy only overlaps with your existing insurance policies that you hopefully already have through your employer or a separate policy. (Remember the list of insurance everyone should have?)

In the event of death, with a standard life insurance policy, the beneficiary of the policy receives the benefit that can be used for any expense they choose, including paying off your shared mortgage. It is typical for financial planners to recommend that a life insurance policy be taken out for an amount that not only covers the lost income of the deceased but for an additional amount to cover other costs. In the case of disability, you would be better off considering a disability insurance policy (similar to life insurance), the benefit from which can be used for more than just your mortgage.

In the end, why pay an additional premium for something that a cost-effective life insurance policy can pay for?

What it comes down to is that this type of policy is very narrow in its coverage and, therefore, is probably not the best use of insurance premiums. You are far better to stick with a good life insurance policy. You can always increase your life insurance coverage to offset your mortgage balance if that is something you are particularly concerned about.

Mortgage vs. Life Insurance

Item	Mortgage Insurance	Life Insurance
Policy Ownership	Bank owns the policy	You own the policy
Beneficiary	Bank is the beneficiary	You choose the beneficiary
Proceeds on death	Bank uses the proceeds to pay for the remaining mortgage	Beneficiaries choose to use the proceeds any way they like
Insurance Rates	Only standard smoker/ non-smoker rate options	Preferred and elite rates make term insurance up to 33% cheaper than mortgage insurance
Underwriting	Post claim underwriting, increasing the risk of a claim being denied	Coverage is underwritten at the time of the application and cannot be denied once approved
Coverage value	Coverage automatically decreases as the mortgage is paid off without any decrease in costs	Coverage can only be decreased by you- any decrease will reduce the cost
Options	Limited options with banks as they only use one carrier	Ability to shop around with multiple carriers for cheaper rates
Selling property/ buying a new home	Insurance ends once house is sold. Need a new mortgage insurance for a new home.	Insurance coverage remains once property is sold. The owner gets the value of the house sold AND keeps their insurance coverage
Guarantees	Banks can increase rates or cancel the coverage on a group basis	Rates and coverage amounts are fully guaranteed once approved

⊙MIRFP

2- Travel and Flight Insurance

Travel and flight insurance policies offer another type of coverage that may just require you to pay a premium for insurance that may overlap with coverage or benefits you already have. First, check your current health and life policies to see how incidents, resulting during travel or flights, are covered.

More than likely, there is some coverage included. Moreover, in the event of some catastrophe, your life insurance policy should provide coverage in the event of your death.

If you use a card to book tickets or travel arrangements, you will also want to check with your credit card company. Many credit card companies automatically provide some basic coverage when they are used to purchase travel tickets. If, after checking these alternative routes, you find that you still need some additional coverage to keep your mind at peace, you can always purchase additional insurance to cover only what you need that is above and beyond what you already have.

3-Cancer Insurance/Disease Insurance

Disease insurance, like cancer insurance, is becoming very popular recently with a rise in cancer rates and overall awareness. However, is it a good idea? While cancer treatment can come with some astronomical medical bills, you might want to hold off on taking out a cancer-specific insurance policy. The reason cancer and disease insurance is such a poor insurance choice is that, in most cases, your primary health insurance policy covers medical expenses related to cancer treatment. If you are worried about the cost of potentially expensive treatments, like cancer treatment, you should start by checking what your current coverage looks like.

Beyond the likely overlap in coverage, the most shocking reason cancer insurance policies can become a waste of money is that most cancer insurance does not even cover skin cancer, the leading type of cancer. Not only that, but cancer insurance typically doesn't even cover outpatient expenses related to the cancer treatment. So what are you paying for?

Unless your health insurance specifically does not cover cancer-related expenses, or you have a high likelihood of getting a specific type of cancer that could be covered by a policy, you are more than likely wasting money on a premium you could be using elsewhere.

Mistakes and Solutions While Getting Insured

1-Choosing Not to Have Basic Insurance

[47]It is essential that you have basic insurance coverage. This is one of the most common financial mistakes that people make.You should make sure that you have adequate coverage for your needs. It is also important to realize that basic insurance will protect your assets and finances from an accident or another damaging situation. However, it is common to make mistakes when it comes to insurance. When it comes to insurance coverage, a mistake can affect you financially.

2-Over-Insuring Yourself

Another common mistake that will cost you is to over-insure yourself. It can be difficult to determine how much basic insurance you need. This is especially true when you consider the liability insurance. You should talk to an insurance agent (usually an independent one is best) about your assets and how best to protect them. When you are younger, you will not need as much insurance, since you do not have as many assets.

3-Under Insuring Yourself

Another common mistake is to under-insure yourself. This can be quite costly when you realize that your basic insurance will not cover needed expenses. You should consider the maximum amount your insurance will pay for each accident. If you have health insurance, you should consider the maximum amount your policy will pay. A million dollars may seem sufficient, but if you were to have cancer or another major illness, the costs of care might exceed that amount.

4-Getting the Wrong Insurance

You may have the wrong types of basic insurance or too many policies. You can waste your money buying policies that you are not likely to use. If you are young, you do not need to get every type of insurance available. You should make sure you understand the policies that you are getting as well. If you understand what you signed up for, you will not be surprised when it comes time to file a claim.

5-Not Shopping Around for a New Policy

It is important that you shop around for a basic insurance policy. You should do this every few years. You can save money by switching to a new policy. Additionally, you should look at policies that offer discounts for where you work or where you went to college. It does not take much time to shop around for insurance policies every two years. This will help you to keep your rate low.

6-Lying on your insurance coverage will lead to trouble at claim time

[48]Lying on your insurance policy is a direct invitation for the company not to pay out your claim.

However, that reality has not stopped one in five Canadians from doing exactly that, according to a new poll from TD Insurance that found 19% of Canadians have not been completely truthful or have omitted information on their application. That is up from 13% in 2011.

So, what's going on? Are Canadians leaving out a few minor details to save some cash and get a cheaper rate? The same survey found 21% of Canadians have canceled insurance to save money.

You need to give full disclosure if you want to make sure your claims are covered.

"It is stretching things and failing to disclose about what is left out on forms. A frequent one, when it comes to life and health insurance, is pre-existing conditions and medication, visits to the doctor, and that sort of thing."

The problem is, if you fail to disclose your diabetes and get hit by a car, it will not matter that the accident had nothing to do with your condition—your beneficiary might still be denied coverage because that bit of information was not disclosed.

"It does not seem to make sense to the consumer, but the fact of the matter is that if you had disclosed that medical condition, we might not have approved you in the first place."

You might not be denied insurance, but the insurance might also specifically not cover you for pre-existing conditions.

Misrepresentations generally fall into three categories. There is the innocent category of: "I forgot," "I did not think it was important," or "I misunderstood the question." The second category is: "I was worried I would not get approved, so I neglected to mention something." The third might be: "I was trying to keep my premiums down a bit."

How to Fix This Mistake

The best thing to do if you have made a mistake, or have a change of heart on what you filled out, is to tell your insurance company. It could mean your policy is now rejected or more expensive, or there may be no impact at all.

With some policy situations, insurance companies don't conduct much due diligence before giving someone a policy. They do a standard questionnaire that is pretty basic, and they do not dig any further. They do not request your medical records or anything like that. It is not until you die that they start looking into it in much detail.

Insurance companies will look for a pattern of misrepresentation on something like whether you have smoked marijuana in the last three years.

In standard policies, there is usually some questionnaire, and each insurance company has a different underwriting procedure. There is a difference between a material representation and a non-material representation.

The key is the amount of due diligence that is done before a policy is approved.

"We have had severe underwriting at death. What I mean by that is something seems suspicious, so they ask for doctor's reports going back ten years. They have not [been] rejected, but they sure have tried."

One of the key differences for consumers is how much due diligence is done by the insurance company before a policy is issued. For travel insurance policies, there is tiny policing beforehand, so when a claim comes in for hundreds of thousands of dollars in medical tests, investigators are dispatched. It is simply too expensive to vet travel policies beforehand.

Finally, the process is the opposite of life policies. "First, they ask you a bunch of questions and, then, they ask your doctor a bunch of questions," and that method is far more likely to discover some oversight. Outright lying will ultimately land you in the most trouble. "It is not worth it. You cannot fix it after you are dead." Visit www.insurecanadian.com for more information.

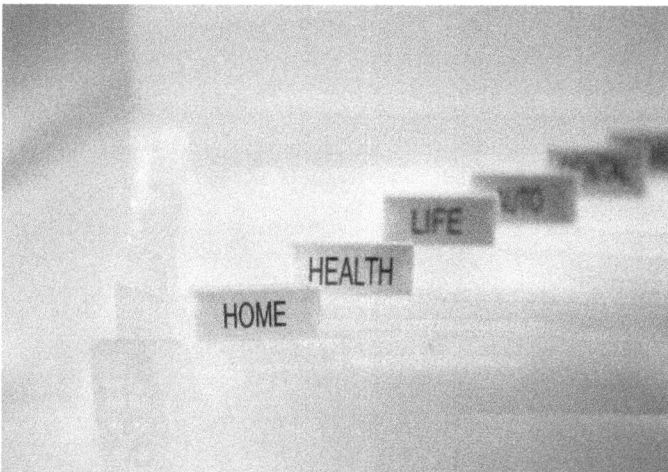

[44] www.sulit.com.ph
[45] www.blue-greenlife.com
[46] www.financialplan.about.com
[47] www.thebalance.com
[48] www.business.financialpost.com

Chapter 7

Change is Life ...
Understanding Life Stages

Chapter 7 – Change is Life...Understanding Life Stages

- Life is Full of Changes
- Single with No Dependents
- Rule of 72 and Computing Effect
- Tying the Knot
- Building a Family
- Just Bought a House
- Single Again
- Nearing Retirement
- Retirement planning and Capital distribution

It's not a matter of
if you should plan
for your future
...it's **when**

Life is full of changes, *and with each new set of circumstances comes new financial needs.*

Any well designed personal financial plan should include life insurance, savings, and investments. Sometimes the lines that separate these three distinct financial products get blurred because particular types of life insurance include savings and investing components. When it comes to planning your budget, examine all three of these categories separately for best results

The main focus in this book is on insurance, but a sound financial plan is based upon insurance and savings.

Let's look at when and why you should buy insurance and start saving.

"A planner can help you determine the best strategy for you. It is not about age; it is about what you want to accomplish."

1 – Single with No Dependents

Insurance

[49]If no one depends on you financially, you usually don't need life insurance. Your untimely death will certainly affect many people, but it will not put them in a financial bind, in most cases. If your parents are not well-off, however, you might consider purchasing a small, inexpensive policy that would cover your funeral and burial costs.

Saving

[50]You are young, and you are broke, thanks to student loans or credit card debt. So, when a financial planner discusses the topic of retirement, you may wonder if the planner lives on a different planet.

"A critical problem for young people is cash flow. However, now is the best time to start saving for that big event. The earlier you start, the better off you will be." At this stage, most financial planners will advise you to participate in your RRSP.Start saving a little for an emergency fund or take advantage of a TFSA.

Rule of 72 and Computing Effect

The Rule of 72 is a simplified way to determine how long an investment will take to double, given a fixed annual rate of interest. By dividing 72 by the annual rate of return, investors can get a rough estimate of how many years it will take for the initial investment to duplicate itself.

For example, the rule of 72 states that $1 invested at 10% would take 7.2 years ((72/10) = 7.2) to turn into $2. In reality, a 10% investment will take 7.3 years to double (($1.10^{7.3} = 2$).

When dealing with low rates of return, the Rule of 72 is fairly accurate. This chart compares the numbers given by the rule of 72 and the actual number of years it takes an investment to double.

2 – Tying the Knot

Insurance

[51]Getting married in and of itself does not mean you need to purchase life insurance. However, events associated with getting married, like buying a house and having children, do mean that you will probably need it soon. Since life insurance gets more expensive as you get older, and since a decline in health could make your policy more expensive, or make you uninsurable, you might want to go ahead and get life insurance when you get married, if you are young and healthy. It is better to buy Term for a larger amount of coverage and have some permanent for a smaller amount, as the premiums will be lower and it will be easy to afford when you are young and healthy.

I will be sharing some illustrations and some success and failure stories at the end, which will make it clearer.

Savings

[52]Married couples have a reputation for fighting mainly about one of two things. For newlyweds, it is likely to be money.With proper financial planning, you get actual professional help with budgeting, setting financial goals, and determining who will pay for what. He or she can also help you study employee benefits and make sure you are not duplicating your efforts.Whatever your goals are, talking through them with a professional and getting a plan down on paper will help you

and your partner work together to reach them. "Tensions always arise because of money." And the solution is a proper financial plan with the division of rules.

3 – Building a Family

Insurance

Perhaps the most important time to have life insurance is during the years when your children rely on you to provide for them. As soon as you know that a child will be entering the picture, you should get life insurance, if you do not have it already. If you or your spouse passes away unexpectedly, the surviving spouse will bear the burden of not only earning an income but also caring for the children.

At this stage in your life, you will want a strong policy that will not only pay for 18 (or more) years of child-rearing expenses but also ongoing household expenses and perhaps college tuition. Make sure to buy enough insurance to allow your family to maintain the same standard of living.

If you already have life insurance at this stage, you should re-evaluate your policy because you might need to purchase more coverage.

4 – Just Bought a House

If you have just bought a house, among the flood of junk mail you will receive will be solicitations for mortgage protection insurance, also called mortgage life insurance. These come in the form of official-looking notices instructing, not asking, you to complete and return a short document requesting personal information such as the borrower and co-borrower's date of birth, sex, tobacco use, occupation, phone numbers, age, and weight. Filling out this form does not usually mean that you are purchasing an insurance policy; it just sets you up to receive sales phone calls to further discuss mortgage protection insurance and perhaps other financial products.

Mortgage protection insurance guards against the loss of income of the person, or people, responsible for paying the mortgage. This is to prevent one catastrophic event from leading to another, like the loss of your family's home. Though it is important to protect against the loss of a breadwinner's income when there are significant household expenses like a mortgage, you would not necessarily need to immediately pay off the mortgage if that person passed away, which is what mortgage protection insurance does. What you would need is cash to cover all of your living expenses. Term life insurance will give you the cash to spend as you see fit.

The only reason to consider mortgage protection insurance instead of term life insurance is if you cannot meet the underwriting criteria for the latter. You may be able to get mortgage protection insurance without passing a medical exam. However, it is also possible to get small amounts of term life insurance without a medical exam, so if you are difficult to insure, a combination of both of these products might be right for you.

Savings

[53]Your beautiful children will surely be brilliant and want to pursue a higher education.The costs of college continue to rise, and if you do not start saving on time, OSAP or other educational loans will be the only option for your children . It is quite difficult for anybody to save the total amount needed for college these days. However, the earlier you start saving for college, the better off you will be.

Parents often need to set up college savings accounts for infants. RESPs can grow tax-free and, as long as funds are used for college expenses, their withdrawal usually will not trigger taxes. A financial planner can help you navigate through RESP plan options.

"The key is to have a discussion and to get started saving because college costs are far and away exceeding inflation."

5 – Single Again

Nobody plans to get divorced but, if you do, your financial situation can change dramatically.

"It is traumatic enough to go through a divorce. However, afterward, most people need help putting themselves back together, mentally and financially. If you wait until years after your divorce to look at your investments, estate planning, and asset protection, sometimes it is too late." Post-divorce planning may involve re-establishing credit, especially if most of the marital assets were in your spouse's name. A financial planner can also help you rethink your budget and retirement plans, and change the beneficiary of your accounts so that your savings will not revert to your ex-spouse.

"There's a lot of busy work that needs to be done."

6 – Nearing Retirement

Insurance

By the time you reach retirement age, your term policy probably will have run out. If you want life insurance when you are older, it will be very expensive—possibly prohibitively expensive. That is because your chances of dying, and the chance that the insurance company will have to pay a death benefit, increase substantially when you are older. In other words, you become a riskier customer, and insurance companies will ask you to pay accordingly.

If you have a whole life policy, it will cover you until you die, but if you no longer need the policy, you may want to terminate it to save the monthly premiums and get full use of your cash value. Some insurance products enable you to participate in the market's upward moves, but avoid its declines.

Savings

Whether or not you have started saving early for retirement, it is crucial at this juncture to determine your retirement readiness.

"Statistically, the most critical time to meet with an adviser is in your late 40s and early 50s, when one, on average, is at his or her peak earning years and accumulating the most retirement assets. Those assets must be properly managed in order to meet retirement goals. A mistake at this stage of one's life will make retirement very unpleasant." A planner can help you eliminate risk in your portfolio and consider investment vehicles such as immediate annuities that offer a guaranteed income for the rest of your life.

Retirement Planning and Capital Distribution

[54]After the asset accumulation and appreciation phase, we then move into the capital distribution phase of our lives,

otherwise known as retirement, around our early to mid 60s. A few years leading up to this point, it is wise to begin to reallocate higher risk assets, such as stocks, into low-risk assets such as bonds. This will help ensure you do not run out of money during retirement.

During the capital distribution phase, many begin to rely on their personal assets, such as savings and social security benefits, to support them financially. In addition to distributing your assets for income purposes, you may also begin to gift additional assets to family members as part of an estate plan.

If you have planned carefully for retirement and avoided any major financial disasters in your working years, you should not need life insurance when you're older. [55]Your retirement accounts and the rest of your nest egg should provide for a surviving spouse's needs. Your mortgage may be paid off, and your children will be old enough to support themselves.

Finally, here's one more tip: if you win the lottery, you might be able to cancel your life insurance policy and stop saving. If you are wealthy enough, you can insure yourself. Otherwise, you will want to re-evaluate your life insurance needs each time your life situation changes significantly, to make sure that anyone who would be financially affected by your death and illness will be taken care of. This means you and your family would be ready for unknown financial disasters.

Visit www.insurecanadian.com for more information.

4 in 10 people buy **Life Insurance** because of a life event

Getting Married   Buying a Home   Having a Baby

[49] www.nigerianobservernews.com
[50] www.bankrate.com/retirement/financial-planning-at-5-stages-of-life
[51] www.investopedia.com/financial-edge/0312/the-best-type-of-life-insurance-for-you-right-now.
[52] www.nigerianobservernews.com
[53] www.nigerianobservernews.com, www.bankrate.com
[54] www.truefinancialplanning.com
[55] www.investopedia.com/financial-edge/0312/the-best-type-of-life-insurance-for-you-right-now

Chapter 8

Why People Say NO ...
Are You Ready to Face the Unknown?

Chapter 8 – Why People Say NO...Are You Ready to Face the Unknown?

"If people understood what life insurance does, we wouldn't need salesmen to sell it. People would come knocking on the door. But they don't understand."

– Ben Feldman

- Debunking the Ten Biggest Myths About Life Insurance
- Unmasking the Biggest Life Insurance Mistakes
- The Shocking Truth
- Other Factors/Assumptions

Debunking the Ten Biggest Myths About Life Insurance

"There's no question that not everyone needs life insurance. There's little reason to buy it if you do not have any dependents, since there is no economic catastrophe associated with death.

Even then, though, there are exceptions. Those who expect family responsibilities soon, may wish to get coverage early to guard against a health change that could raise costs. Substantial term life insurance is inexpensive for young non-smokers, so paying for what you do not need yet, but will soon, is not a serious burden."

[56]Still, at least the case can be made that if you are single, and especially if you are single as well as relatively young and healthy, you may not feel a pressing need to purchase life insurance as soon as possible.

The same can't be said for a lot of the excuses that people who pass on buying this type of insurance use when asked to explain their hesitation or indifference. In fact, most of the reasons cited by folks who fail to see the appeal or benefit of life insurance are pretty easily refutable, with the following examples being noteworthy cases in point.

When learning to speak, often one of the first words to come out of a child's mouth is the word *no*. Moreover, after that day, they learn to know the word pretty well. For better or worse, people do not grow out of their use of the word *no*. While you may hear the word more than you would like in the business of sales, by asking right questions and getting to the root of the obstacle, you may be able to turn that *no* into a *yes*.

First, let's point out that while *no* doesn't always mean *no*, sometimes it does. It is important to identify those instances since using irritating or pushy practices rarely garners favor with consumers. Your job is to be helpful and connect them with solutions that fit their needs. It starts with asking good, probing questions to identify that need and discover what the real emotion is behind the *no*. According to renowned author and salesman, Zig Ziglar, each sale has five basic obstacles: no need; no money; no hurry; no desire; and no trust. Here are some ways to speak to each of them:

Following are the 10 main reasons people do not buy Life Insurance. Many people could benefit from a life insurance policy but still choose not to purchase one. Learn why they should give life insurance another look:

1. Life insurance costs too much (or I cannot afford it)

Here's the funny thing about this particular line of reasoning: usually life insurance is not all that expensive.

That depends on some factors, of course, including how old you are when you decide to take out a policy, how healthy (or unhealthy) you are at that time, whether or not you are a smoker, which type of life insurance, and how much coverage you want to buy.

If you are fairly young and healthy and you are not a smoker, though, you should be able to get a 20-year, $250,000 level-term policy for less than $200 annually.

This is far from common knowledge among today's consumers; though, I suggest that "consumers do not have a good understanding of how much a life policy might cost. In fact, they tend to over-estimate the actual cost a lot," with a good example being that a recent study showed when asked to guess the yearly cost of the policy mentioned above, the average person replied $400. The median response from people under the age of 25, on the other hand, was $600, while a whopping one in four assumed the bill to come to $1,000 or more.

2. I do not need it because I have plenty of assets to leave my loved ones

That may be true, but what form are those assets in at the moment? Are they mainly liquid, meaning your beneficiaries could quickly convert them into cash should the need arise? Alternatively, are they mostly in non-liquid form, which would mean real estate, a share in business, or even jewelry?

If it's the latter, a life insurance policy could provide your loved ones with access to some *ready cash* that would allow them to pay off debts that require immediate attention and also let them retain those non-liquid assets rather than potentially sell them for a fraction of what they'd get if they could hold on to them for a while longer.

3. I am healthy

You are now, but what about five or 10 years down the road? None of us knows for sure how healthy—or not—we are going to be tomorrow or the next day, let alone a year or a decade in the future.

It does not take much Internet surfing to find stories of people who ignored life insurance because they were healthy or young (or both), only to be blindsided by an unexpected medical crisis that made them ineligible for life insurance.

This doesn't mean everyone should run out and buy as much life insurance as he or she can afford. If you have a spouse, or children, or a parent who relies on your financial support, though, you should seriously consider at least some form and amount of life insurance, even if you regularly get clean bills of health from your physician.

4. I have too many other things to worry about right now

Maybe you are recently married, or you are busy prepping for your trip down the aisle. Alternatively, maybe you are about to have a baby, or you just had one.

Those situations, and much more, have prompted many people to put *buying life insurance* at the bottom of their to-do lists—assuming it ever made it onto these lists to begin with.

As was mentioned earlier, though, you never know when something unfortunate or unexpected could happen to you, so if there are people in your life who depend on your income, you should make life insurance a priority again as soon as you are able.

This situation, also called *present-day bias*, means we tend to put the needs of today over those of the future. "Today is always more important than tomorrow, but life insurance is all about protecting the future."

Young people think of death as something that won't happen to the —at least, not soon—so they do not plan for it. Today's needs are more pressing than this seemingly remote future event.

5. I do not understand it well enough to buy it

All sorts of studies have found that one of the main reasons people do not purchase life insurance is that they are confused by all of the varieties and options that are made available to them during the buying process.

In a recent study, for example, 38 percent of participants cited "I am not sure how much or what type to buy" as their reason for not purchasing.

"Given that buying life insurance is believed to be important and not something that is often done, the uncertainty that surrounds it paralyzes many people."

One fairly obvious solution to this issue is to reach out to an experienced agent so you can be led through the process by a helping hand rather than tackle it on your own.

6. I find the process intimidating

According to a recent study, more than 70 percent of people who purchased life insurance policies through their employer said they were happy with the process and even described it as *comfortable.*

A more recent study from the same organization, on the other hand, suggested that those who go to buy life insurance on their own are far less pleased with the experience. In fact, many say they find it *intimidating.*

Again, this is another situation where working with a professional who knows the ins and outs of the industry would help ease some of the tension associated with such a complex product.

7. I have other financial obligations that are more important than life insurance

For some people, spending their hard-earned cash on vacations, or shopping, movies, or eating out, is more important than using it to pay for a life insurance policy. For others, cable, the Internet, and phone bills come before life insurance.

In fact, in a recent study, 60 percent of Millennials consider their cellphone, the Internet, and cable payments higher priorities than purchasing life insurance, with 49 percent of those 65 and older saying the same thing.

Consumers today are confronted with more financial demands than ever. Younger shoppers, in particular, realize they need life insurance, but it is not a priority for them.

One way to make it more of a priority for younger and older consumers alike is to reinforce just how cheap life insurance can be—especially if you spend a bit less on eating out, movies, or even your daily coffee run, and use the savings to fund an insurance policy instead.

8. I do not trust insurance companies or agents

This keeps more people than you may imagine from buying life insurance, A study conducted found that nearly 40 percent of respondents have refrained from it due to the apprehension they feel for insurance agents.

If this describes you, there are some places you can go to read up on any companies you are considering doing business with, with A.M. Best, the Better Business Bureau, the National Association of Insurance Commissioners, and your state insurance commissioner's office, being four great examples.

9. I will get to it eventually

Another way of putting the above is to say that many people procrastinate when it comes to purchasing a life insurance policy.

"Even though they recognize the value of life insurance and are aware of their need for it, many consumers (30 percent, according to the most recent Insurance Barometer Study) just haven't gotten around to taking care of that need."

10. It makes me think about death

Similarly, 30 percent of the men and women who participated in the 2015 Insurance Barometer Study suggested they have avoided buying life insurance because doing so causes them to think about their mortality.

Unfortunately, there's no easy way to combat this particular quandary—other than, perhaps, to point out that the thought of leaving your spouse, or children, or other loved ones in dire financial straits, is not likely to be much more, if at all, appealing than thinking about passing away.

Unmasking the Biggest Life Insurance Mistakes

In what kinds of situations or circumstances would I want to avoid or ignore life insurance?

Most experts will suggest staying away from life insurance if you are single, or if you do not have any dependents. Many will say the same regarding retirees—or at least a certain segment of the retired population. There are times when even folks in these situations may want to buy life insurance, though—with two cases in point being young, single people who assist siblings or parents, and retirees who help support grandchildren.

Do empty nesters need life insurance?

Sometimes, yes. For example, are there people in your life who depend on you for financial assistance? If so, you will probably want to invest in this kind of insurance even if your children have *flown the coop*. Another instance when life insurance may make sense for a so-called empty nester is if you are all at once in a *blackout* period that impacts some folks—women, especially—following the death of a spouse.

I am a retiree. Do I still need life insurance?

Whether or not you *need* life insurance as a retiree depends on your current circumstances. If you are free of debt, you no longer rely on an occupation for income, you have children who are self-sufficient, or if you are having trouble paying your premiums, you very well may not need, or no longer need it. That said, if you are still paying off your house, or if you are supporting one or more dependents—a good example would be grandchildren you may be caring for, or even adult children who are disabled—you could make a far worse purchase than life insurance

The Shocking Truth

"It is too expensive!" The No. 1 Reason People Do Not Buy Life Insurance and Why They Are Wrong

"It is too expensive!" is the common refrain when Americans are asked why they do not get the life insurance protection they need. However—and it is a big but—*"80% overestimate how much it costs."*

2015 INSURANCE BAROMETER STUDY

The True Cost of LIFE INSURANCE

3 out of 4 of people say they have a **good understanding** of life insurance

But do they, really?

When it comes to cost... they don't!

When asked how much the yearly cost would be for a 20-year $250,000 level term life insurance policy for a healthy 30-year-old:

80%
Overestimated the cost

They guessed **$400** a year

Those **under 25**, who tend to pay the least for coverage, said **$600** a year

And **1** in **4** thought it would be **$1,000** a year or more!

BUT...

The true cost for that $250,000 policy is about $160 a year. That's a little over **40¢** a day or **$13** a month[1].

To put it into perspective,

Here's what the cost looks like compared with what many people spend per month on:

$13	$61	$64	$80	$140
life insurance	cell phone[2]	cable TV[3]	coffee on the way to work[4]	take-out lunch[5]

Trimming just a few dollars from any of these would make getting—*and affording* —life insurance a no-brainer.

Learn more at www.lifehappens.org/barometer

LIFE HAPPENS. LIMRA
A NONPROFIT ORGANIZATION

SOURCES:
All data is from the 2015 Insurance Barometer Study by Life Happens and LIMRA, unless otherwise noted.
[1] Life insurance quote is from Quick Life Center, quoted in April 2015.
[2] New Street Research, The Wall Street Journal, March 3, 2014.
[3] Report on Cable Industry Prices, Federal Communications Commission, May 16, 2014.
[4,5] Accounting Principals' Workonomix Survey, conducted by Braun Research, 2013.

"Over the last five years, a study shows that consumers think life insurance is more expensive than it is We need to help educate the public about how affordable life insurance can be."

Other Factors/Assumptions:

Religion and culture:

In some faiths, people assume it is against God's will to buy insurance, as there is interest factor involved and it means you do not trust God. How can it be wrong to prepare yourself for future financial loss, and to make sure you and your family's integrity is never compromised?

Group Insurance

Sometimes people assume they are covered by their group insurance plans; they need to understand the coverage and benefits that are being offered, as most of the time they are not enough. There are no medical tests performed, so they are not customized and very basic.Understand your need and fill the gap of insurance needed.

Covered through OHIP

Most of the time it has been seen that people assume they are covered by OHIP (Ontario Health Insurance Program)for everything, whereas it is not true. OHIP covers very basic medical needs; in some cases, you need out of province health insurance, as it has restrictions if you are in a province other than the one you are a resident of.

Sharing a few links to understand OHIP better:

www.health.gov.on.ca/en/public/programs/**ohip**/**ohip**faq_mn.a spx

*settlement.org/.../**health/ohip**...**health-insurance**/...**health-insurance**...**ohip**/does-**ohip**-co...*

*https://www.**health**quotes.ca/**OHIP**-Ontario.aspx*

*settlement.org/ontario/health/**ohip**-and...**ohip**/what-services-does-**ohip**-cover/*

Disability Benefits:

There is also assumption that, if you became disabled, the government will take care of all your expenses, *the same way we assume we are going to get enough at our retirement in Old Age Security. Please do some research and understand the criteria and limits.*

Even if you are paying for CPP, there are exclusions and limitations.

Visit the Government website for details:
https://www.canada.ca/en/services/benefits/**disability**.html

Insurance Scams

If someone close to you has been going through some insurance scam, or a company didn't pay an insurance claim, you assume it's all a scam but, normally, scammers are in every industry. Also, if you have lied on your insurance application to hide material facts at the allegation time, they will refuse to pay you, as at the date of investigation they will find out the truth and will return your premiums.

Financial Education at schools

Financial literacy is critical. Canadian education systems should add a subject on financial planning for high school students, which should teach the basics of savings, investing, and insurance. They should know how a mortgage works, how to use a credit card and a line of credit, how compound interest and the Rule of 72 works, and how to maintain their credit history, etc.

[57]Realizing this fact, the Government of Canada has named November as *Financial Literacy Month*, a month to empower Canadians with the knowledge, skills, and confidence to make responsible financial decisions. Financial literacy, among other things, is insurance literacy. Insurance literacy can help consumers better protect their homes, cars, and businesses, while keeping their costs under control.

Non Medical/Simplified Issue Insurance Plans

If someone has severe health issues, or a bad family medical history, it is assumed they are not insurable; whereas, in most of cases, there are still a few plans which will cover them, but the premium will be higher than regular plans. For example, Simplified Issue or Non-medical Life Insurance plans [58]still have a host of health-related questions. You should also keep in mind that the face amount on these policies is often limited coverage because it's necessary for a life insurance company to set a maximum to cover potential losses.The chance of an insurance company receiving a claim for a life insurance policy that requires no medical exam is much greater than from a traditional policy.

Under traditional insurance plans, you complete a regular medical exam and (if you're in very good health and your family has a very good medical history) you can be approved at preferred rates or standard rates. If you are deemed to have a health risk, you will be rated (charged extra) and, in those cases where your health risk is deemed too severe to qualify for the policy, declined.

Finally: How Your Subconscious Keeps You from Buying Life Insurance

When we are thinking logically, we know we should buy life insurance, yet so many of us don't.

When asked about it, people say it costs too much, or they do not have time to sort through its complexities. However, those may just be excuses cooked up by the subconscious, according to a new study.

"A lot of our decision-making is often unconscious; people often can't tell us why they do what they do."

Visit www.insurecanadian.com *for more information.*

[56] www.quotewizard.com, www.northamericancompany.com
[57] www.financialliteracyinfo.ca
[58] www.firstchoicefinancialgroup.ca

Chapter 9

7 K's of Getting Insured Right

Chapter 9 – 7 K's of Getting Insured Right

13 K's Of Choosing an Advisor

Golden Tips

We have established that insurance is the base of a financial plan .We have understood the types of plans available, the policies one must have and those one doesn't need, the importance of savings as compared to insurance, and the types of Insurance we need at different stages of life.For peace of mind, we should have proper coverage that is only possible by knowing these seven factors.

- Know your insurance needs
- Know the right amount of insurance
- Know your budget
- Know your market
- Know your insurance specialist
- Know your contract
- Know your follow up process

1. Know Your Insurance Needs

6 common uses for your life insurance benefit

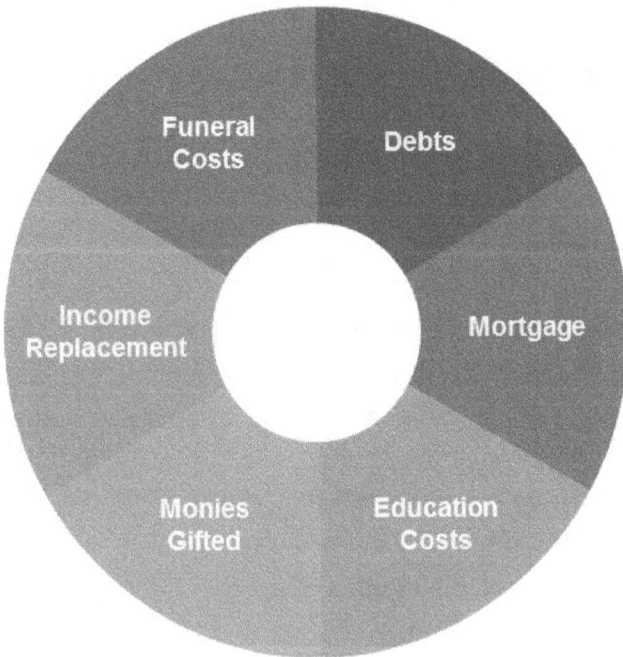

[59]The first step is to establish the need for insurance. Ask yourself: do you need insurance, and how much do you need? Which life stage are you at?

Your insurance needs should be based on your family, age, and economic situation. There are many forms of insurance and, unfortunately, no one-size-fits-all policy. Life insurance, for example, can be a virtual necessity, especially if you have a spouse and children. Disability insurance, which provides an income stream if you are unable to work, is important for everyone.

Most people require some amount of all of these categories of insurance.

[60]The most obvious reason why people need life insurance is to protect their dependents. However, there are other equally important reasons why you might want to have life insurance:

- To cover taxes at death on liquid assets
- To pay off debts
- To meet final expenses like funeral expenses, lawyer, and executor fees
- To provide income for your dependents
- To leave a larger estate for your beneficiaries
- To create a pool of cash to allow your executor to make things equal for your beneficiaries when some things cannot be divided

- To help corporations and business arrangements remain viable
- To help businesses cope with the loss of key people.

Obviously, this list is not exhaustive, but it does represent some of the key uses of life insurance.

You need a competent *Insurance Specialist* to go through all your current expenses, income, assets, and liabilities to determine the amount of coverage you need.

2. Know the Right Amount of Insurance

Once you know why you need insurance, you then need to know the right amount of insurance. This is one of the most important steps in planning for life insurance. Determining the right amount is not always easy. We think it is more of an art than a science. You need enough to meet your goals, but you do not necessarily want to buy more than you need. When in doubt, get help from a professional advisor.

Living Insurance

Life insurance contracts are an unselfish benefit because it is really the beneficiaries that benefit when you die. Living insurance is a more selfish type of insurance because it pays you before you die. Two good examples of this are Long Term Care Insurance and Critical Illness Insurance.

You need a competent *Insurance Specialist* to go through all your current expenses, income, assets, and liabilities to determine the amount of coverage you need as death and living benefits.

3. Know Your Budget

The next issue to consider is the appropriate type of life insurance to use. [61]Which type of insurance is best for you? The answer is found in your reason for buying insurance in the first place. For example, if you want insurance to pay off your mortgage so your family is not burdened with debt, then term insurance is probably all you need. On the other hand, if you want insurance to create a bigger estate for your heirs, then a permanent policy is probably more appropriate.

Basically, there are two kinds of life insurance: temporary insurance and permanent insurance.

Another name for temporary insurance is term insurance. Term insurance is the most cost-effective type of insurance. It is designed to protect you for only a temporary period. As you get older, term insurance gets more expensive. Once you reach 70 or 80 years of age, you will not be able to get any term insurance coverage.

The second type of insurance is permanent insurance. Permanent insurance stays in force until you die. As long as you pay the premiums, your permanent life insurance policy remains an asset in your estate planning. The benefit with permanent insurance is a price that is fixed over your lifetime, unlike term insurance where the price increases as you get older. There are three basic types of permanent insurance: Term to 100, Whole Life, and Universal Life.

In short, everyone would love to have permanent plans which will not expire till death but, of course, the premium for such plans is very high, and not everyone can afford it.For most people, term insurance, or the combination of term plus permanent insurance, is the best solution; it will be in the budget and provide the required coverage.

A good advisor can design a ladder plan that will exactly match the need of insurance with different stages of life.With a few insurance companies, you will also receive a multi-coverage discount as well by having ladder plan, having a couple insured under one policy, or by having a combination of life and living benefits under one plan.

4. Know Your Market

Just like anything else in life, not all life insurance products are created equally. That is particularly the case when it comes to price. Once you have an idea of what type of life insurance you need and how much you need, it is crucial to shop around for the best deal. If you are not sure how to accomplish that, then seek advice from an independent insurance broker who can shop around for you.

5. Know Your Insurance Specialist

"A good Advisor is the one who doesn't just sell   life insurance; HE SELLS WHAT LIFE INSURANCE CAN DO FOR YOU."

When looking for an advisor, choose one who is giving you advice, not selling you something, and one who is open about conflicts of interest.

This is the most important step ,to choose the right advisor, who will help you to understand the amount of insurance you need as per your budget.

[62]Selecting a good, independent insurance agent to take care of your insurance needs should not be an *eeny, meeny, miny, moe* decision. You are looking for a long-term relationship with someone you can trust. You would not buy a car without shopping around, and you should not select an independent agent without also doing some research. So, what should you look for?

[63]Because your financial professional understands your needs, as well as the role of the various kinds of insurance within an individual financial picture, he or she can help you with the policies that are most appropriate for you. Your financial professional can provide you with costs and complete details.

[64]One might think choosing an insurance agent should be an easy task: pick the one that offers you the lowest price, right?

Well, that is not necessarily the case and probably shouldn't be at the top of your list of priorities when choosing the best agent. A lower price can mean inferior coverage, and that is fine until you experience a loss that isn't covered.

6. Know Your Contract

[65]Almost all of us have insurance. When your insurer gives you the policy document, all you do is glance over the decorated words in the policy and pile it up with the other bunch of commercial papers on your desk, right? If you spend thousands of dollars each year on insurance, don't you think that you should know all about it? Your insurance advisor is always there for you to help you understand the tricky terms in the insurance forms, but you should also know for yourself what your contract says. In this article, we'll make reading your insurance contract easy. Read on to take a look at the basic principles of insurance contracts and how they are put to use in daily life.

Essentials of a Valid Insurance Contract

Offer and Acceptance

When applying for insurance, the first thing you do is get the proposal form of a particular insurance company. After filling in the requested details, you send the form to the business (sometimes with a premium check). This is your offer. If the insurance company accepts your offer and agrees to insure you, this is called acceptance. In some cases, your insurer may agree to accept your offer after making some changes to your proposed terms (for example, charging you a double premium for your chain-smoking habit).

Consideration

This is the premium, or the future premiums, that you have pay to your insurance company. For insurers, consideration also refers to the money paid out to you should you file an insurance claim. This means that each party to the contract must provide some value to the relationship.

Legal Capacity

You need to be legally competent to enter into an agreement with your insurer. If you are a minor or are mentally ill, for example, then you may not be qualified to make contracts. Similarly, insurers are considered to be competent if they are licensed under the prevailing regulations that govern them.

Legal Purpose: If the purpose of your contract is to encourage illegal activities, it is invalid.

7. Know Your Follow-up Process

You should be clear enough after buying insurance that it is not some perishable goods. Review your policy at least once a year, or if there is any major change in your life. You should also understand your current life stage. In short, your financial plan should be updated whenever there are any major changes in your life. Again, it's the responsibility of your insurance agent to make you understand the importance of the follow-up process.He should be in touch with you at least once a year. Your agent should also be keeping you up to date on relevant regulations, new laws, changes in your career, and anything else that might affect you as the end customer.

13 K's of choosing an advisor

Here are 13 things you should consider when choosing an insurance agent:

1. Direct Writers vs. Independent Agents
2. What type of insurance do you need?
3. Decide If location Is important to you
4. Technical knowledge and credentials
5. Visit their websites
6. Personality traits
7. Knowledge and trust are key
8. Questions to ask
9. Do your homework
10. Expectations
11. Detailed written proposals
12. What to expect after binding coverage
13. Time change—stay active with your insurance coverages

Direct Writers vs. Independent Agents: There are two different ways to get coverage from an insurance company.

Direct writers are insurance companies that hire their sales people to write exclusively for that one company; they work for the enterprise that employs them. Independent agents work for the insured, not the company. However, they have contracts with multiple insurance companies and can usually offer you more options.

What type of insurance do you need? Some agents will offer many types of insurance, and some will be limited in their offerings. For example, some might only offer personal lines insurance, whereas others will provide both personal and commercial lines. If you own a business and are looking for an agent to write your commercial insurance, you want to make sure they have some experience in your industry.

.

[66]**Decide if location is important to you:** It may be substantial for you that your independent agent has offices in your community. You have the convenience of being able to stop by to ask questions or get help with a claim, and to develop a trusting relationship. Many independent agents are deeply committed to their community and are actively involved as coaches, scout leaders, or civic leaders.

Technical knowledge and credentials: You should always ask the agent about their experience before trusting them as your insurance advisor. One indication of their technical knowledge is if they have letters after their name. These letters stand for professional insurance designations that signify a higher level of experience and competence. A knowledgeable independent agent can provide the advice you need when deciding what coverage and limits you need to protect your family and yourself. Look for independent agents who have letters next to their name on their business card. These represent professional designations, such as Certified Financial Planner Insurance(CFP), Chartered Property and Casualty Underwriter (CPCU), Certified Life Underwriter(CLU), or Certified Health Specialist(CHS).To maintain these credentials, independent agents must take continuing education classes.

Visit their websites: Websites are full of information. Read about the history of the agency, the staff's bios, and their customer testimonials. See if their website provides insurance information and easy access to price quotes, either online or via telephone. Websites can give you a feel for the personality of the agency, what they think is important, and the type of customer service they provide.

Personality traits: Agents get paid commissions by the insurance company, so it is important to find one that is honest and trustworthy. They also should be passionate and enthusiastic about what they do and, of course, you should like your agent. It is much easier to do business with people we like than with people we do not. Personality is important since you should like the agent you are going to work with, potentially for several years. You should feel respect for their knowledge and get a sense of their integrity.

Knowledge and trust are key: It is not so simple to determine knowledge and trust because these qualities are established over time. However, you can start by asking the independent agents, whom you are considering, to explain the products they sell and how they determine which products, coverage, and limits you need. This will give you a good feel.

[67]**Questions to ask:** It is okay to ask questions when looking for an agent. In fact, you should be asking questions when deciding whom you want to work with. Some good questions are:

- What are your areas of expertise?
- What is your reach? Are you local? Statewide? Nationwide?
- What is your experience in my industry? How many years have you been writing this type of insurance?
- Do you have any client references?
- How long have you been in business?
- How many companies do you represent? Which ones?

Do your homework: Before selecting an agent, you should first do your homework on the agent as well as the agency they're associated with. Your first step is to google the agent's name and agency. [68]Are there any news articles about them? Have they faced any lawsuits? Are there any reviews? Have a look at their website. Is it professional? Are there any testimonials? You may also want to check their social media pages (Facebook, LinkedIn, Google+, Twitter, Instagram) for reviews and educational content.

Expectations: A good way to gauge if the agent can live up to your expectations is by asking them for a quote before you commit to doing business with them. This should give you a good idea of how efficient they are (how fast they can get you a quote), how thorough they are when explaining what coverage you are afforded in the policy, and why the price varies if more than one quote is provided.

Detailed written proposals: Once your agent gets quotes for your business, you should review them carefully. There are different types of carriers, and coverages can vary dramatically. Some carriers may have exclusions on their policies removing extensive coverages. Make sure you work with the agent to ensure you have the coverage you need, even if that means paying a little more.

What to expect after binding coverage: Your agent's job is not done once you have bound coverage, and your expectations of them should not end there either. Customer service is what is going to separate a good agent from a great agent. Say you purchased a new piece of equipment, built a new structure, or underwent renovations—all of these things, along with many others, can affect your insurance policy. Your agent should be checking in with you periodically throughout the year to ask about any changes that might affect your policy. Your agent should be one that is approachable and reachable at all times because, when things do happen, that is when you will need them most.

Times change—stay active with your insurance coverages: As mentioned above, you need to stay active with your insurance coverage because things do evolve over time. Your agent should also be keeping you up to date on relevant regulations, new laws, changes with your career, and anything else that might affect you as the end customer.

Visit **www.**insurecanadian.com for more information.

Golden Tips

- Consider buying a *break point* level of insurance coverage— better premium rates are given at coverage levels of $100,000, $250,000, $500,000 and $1,000,000.
- Make sure you obtain an illustration for the policy that you have chosen. If the insurer does not provide you with one, look for another insurance company.
- Always shop for a level-premium policy. Nobody likes a surprise increase in his or her premium payments! So, before you buy term or permanent insurance, make sure your illustration shows that your premium payment is guaranteed not to increase throughout the duration of your coverage.
- Don't be sold on permanent insurance for the investment or cash value feature. For the first two to 10 years, your premiums are paying the agent's commission anyway. Most policies do not start to build decent cash value until their 12th year, so ask yourself if the feature is worth it.
- Determine your desired duration of coverage so that you purchase the correct type of policy and keep your premium

payments affordable. If you only need insurance for ten years, then buy term. Also, check out multiple, quality insurance companies for their rates.

- Make sure that your insurance carrier has the financial stability to pay your claim in the event of your death.
- Don't be taken with riders. A very few number of policies ever pay under these riders, so avoid things like the accidental death and waiver of premium riders since they will only jack up your premiums.
- For 24 hours before your medical exam, keep sugar and caffeine out of your system. It is best to schedule your exam early in the morning and not to consume anything but water for at least eight hours beforehand.
- If your premiums are much too high due to medical reasons, or you are denied coverage, check if a group plan is available through your company. These group plans require no medical exam or physical.

[59] www.axa-equitable.com
[50] www.retirehappy.ca
[51] www.aliko-aapayrollservices.com
[52] www.batesins.com
[53] www.axa-equitable.com
[54] www.hospitality-mutual.com
[55] www.knowledgefinancial.com
[66] www.batesins.com
[67] www.taleflake.eu.org
[68] www.monitor.co.ug

Chapter 10

Life Insurance as an Estate Planning Tool

Chapter 10 – Life Insurance as an Estate Planning Tool

- Using life insurance for estate planning purposes
- Tax sheltered investing using life insurance
- Life insurance solves other tax problems
- Three common estate costs
- Five ways to manage estate costs
- Probate fees and life insurance
- Cooperation as the owner of an insurance policy
- Insurance as an insured annuity
- Insurance as a legacy

[69]Two facts stand out when it comes to insurance. One, Canadians rarely think about it. Two, there's a good chance they do not have enough of it.

Polls and industry statistics consistently find a significant percentage of us do not have enough basic life insurance to support loved ones in the event of an unexpected calamity.

Canadians also seem to ignore the fact that insurance can be a wealth-management and estate-planning tool.

Using insurance to pile up wealth, or pass it on to the next generation, works best for those who are already in great shape financially. That means people who have excess money to invest after maximizing their tax shelters such as registered retirement savings plans, tax-free savings accounts, and registered education savings plans.

Typically, people put that excess cash into fixed-income investments such as guaranteed investment certificates and bonds. While such investments are extremely safe, they are also highly taxed.

Using Life Insurance for Estate Planning Purposes

[70]Some common reasons you may wish to use life insurance include:
- To provide liquidity in an estate to pay off liabilities such as taxes or mortgages. This will ensure that non-liquid assets,

such as a cottage or business, do not have to be sold, but can be left to your beneficiaries.

- To establish a fund to provide income for an individual you wish to support.
- To make a donation to charity.

While term life insurance can be used to fund a short-term estate need such as paying off an outstanding mortgage or protecting the estate against an immediate shortfall, universal or whole life insurance is the preferred option when the insurance is for estate purposes.

Examples include having a life insurance policy that would cover estate taxes on death (capital gains generated due to the deemed disposition rules) or the ability to leave bequests without the advent of taxes payable.

As with all insurance products that are used for estate planning purposes, a thorough cost-benefit analysis should be performed to assess the appropriateness of the strategy.

Protect your income

While a will and POAs can dictate your wishes, they will not actually take care of your family should you become incapacitated, or die. For that, you'll need insurance.

Life insurance can play different roles, depending on your life stage. "For a young family with a big mortgage, safety and security might be their prime objective. For someone later in life, however, life insurance may be used as an estate planning tool—an opportunity to leave a legacy or pay taxes, so your heirs do not have to."

Using term insurance:

For young families, where money is tight, the most cost-effective option is term life insurance. This type of policy pays out a lump sum should you die during the term, which is usually 10 to 20 years. Usually much cheaper than other options, the one drawback is that term life must be renewed when the term ends, usually at a much higher cost. It is best to buy these policies as early as possible, say in your 20s, as health problems later in life might make you uninsurable.

You'll need to purchase enough coverage to pay off your current debts and replace your future earning potential. The rule of thumb is to purchase a policy that covers 80% of your annual income for the next 10 to 20 years. If you make $50,000 a year and have a $200,000 mortgage, the policy should pay out between $600,000 to $1,000,000.

Using permanent insurance:

The other option is permanent life insurance (including whole life and universal life), which has no expiry date. These policies may have an investment component, which isn't subject to tax, as well as a *cash surrender value,* should you cancel them.

The disadvantage is that they are significantly more expensive in the early years. For example, a 35-year-old, non-smoking male, who opts for $500,000 in coverage, would pay about $35 a month for a term policy; the same universal life policy would cost about $190 a month, and a comparable whole life policy could easily top $250 per month.

Because of the higher cost in the early years, permanent insurance is not the best option for young parents on a budget. However, if you plan on using life insurance to pay estate taxes or leave a legacy, then permanent insurance may be appropriate.

Tax Sheltered Investing Using Life Insurance

Strategies To Use

Irrevocable Life Insurance Trusts

[71]If you and your spouse have a net worth of more than $4 million, take a look at an irrevocable life insurance trust (ILIT).

You make a cash gift to the ILIT to purchase a permanent survivorship life insurance policy. The ILIT is the owner and beneficiary of the policy. When the survivor dies, your heirs will not have to pay estate and income taxes on the death benefits.

Give It Away Now

If you're of more modest means and would like to see your money working for your heirs while you're still alive, as well as increase the amount they will receive when you die, then you might want to consider giving cash to them today.

For the greatest benefit, your heirs can use part of the gift to buy a life insurance policy on your life. Meanwhile, you'll be able to watch your loved ones enjoy the remainder of the money right now.

What's more, you'll reduce your taxable estate by the amount of your gift. And, because your loved ones are the owners and beneficiaries of the policy, they won't have to worry about estate or income taxes on the death benefit when you die. They also won't have to worry about paying income taxes on the growth of the policy's cash value while you're living.

Life Insurance Solves Other Tax Problems

Asset Allocation

There are several versions of permanent life insurance. Some, such as universal life (UL), pay a fixed interest rate on the cash within the policy. Others, however, such as variable universal life (VUL), offer dozens of investment options. These might include a large-cap stock fund, an international stock fund, a bond fund, or even a real estate fund. The list is nearly endless.

The growth of the cash value in VUL is determined by the performance of the underlying portfolio(s). This becomes part of your total investment portfolio. Reallocations within the policy are not taxable. So, when it comes time to rebalance your investments, you will not have to worry about paying income tax on profits you take as you make changes in the VUL.

Maxed Out Retirement Plans

If you contributed the maximum amount to your RRSP and TFSA this year, it is important to know there are no restrictions on how much you can put into permanent life insurance. Plus, you'll at least gain the advantage of tax-deferred growth, and you'll leverage the value of your estate.

Remember, however, that if you later take cash of out the policy, you'll have to pay taxes on it at your ordinary tax rate. So, don't look at this as a substitute for a cash emergency fund. That said, the policy might have a loan provision that lets you borrow from your cash value and thus avoid the tax.

Shelter From Higher Taxes

If you think that income and estate taxes will skyrocket, permanent life insurance can help you transfer wealth into a safe haven that protects your assets from higher taxation.

Pennies on the Dollar

If income and estate taxes keep you awake at night, life insurance might be the answer. Permanent life insurance is one of the most powerful tax planning tools you can find. It offers several unique ways to address your estate tax and income tax liabilities while resolving those tax issues for pennies on the dollar.

Three Common Estate Costs

[72]Planning can help cover or minimize estate costs you may not have considered.

When you die, your debts must be paid first, before any money or property you leave behind is passed on to your loved ones. There may also be funeral costs, legal fees, and other administrative expenses in settling your estate. Moreover, there may be other estate costs, such as probate fees and taxes on investments, that you may not have considered.

1. Probate fees

When you die, your executor often needs proof (requested by financial institutions, government agencies, and others) that they are the person authorized to represent your estate. Probate is the process that provides court certification of this fact. There can be a cost to this, and probate fees to settle your estate can be high depending on the province you live in. In Ontario, the fees (officially called an estate administration tax) equal almost 1.5% of your estate's value.

2. Tax on capital gains

You're deemed to dispose of all assets at death. Your estate must cover the tax on any capital gains.

3. Tax on tax-sheltered savings plans

Registered plans such as RRSPs and RRIFs can be transferred tax-free to your spouse's plan. If you do not have a husband, these savings are fully taxable at your death.

Five Ways to Manage Estate Costs

1. Leave a valid will

If you die without a valid will, your estate gets settled according to the laws of your province, rather than according to your personal wishes. This can be a more complicated process, with higher legal fees, and the potential for costly disputes.

2. Name beneficiaries for insurance and registered plans

When you buy life insurance, or open an RRSP or other registered plan accounts, you can designate a beneficiary to receive the money when you die. This means the money bypasses the estate process and is paid directly to that person.

Because it does not form part of your estate, the money is not subject to probate fees, and there is no delay in your beneficiaries receiving the money.

3. Jointly owned property

Holding assets—such as a home or cottage—with another person is another strategy for reducing probate fees. Joint assets pass automatically to the surviving joint owner and are not considered part of your estate and subject to probate fees.

However, there can be complications to joint ownership, especially if you co-own an asset with someone other than your spouse. For example:

If you transfer half-ownership of an asset to an adult child, and they have a spouse who they later separate from, the spouse could have a claim on your child's half of the asset.

If your child has financial problems or declares bankruptcy, their ownership in the asset could be subject to claims by creditors.

If the asset has increased in value, you may have to pay tax on any capital gains when you transfer your half ownership. This is because a transfer is considered a sale for tax purposes.

You can no longer deal freely with the asset and must make joint decisions in managing or selling it.

Professional advice is essential

Joint ownership arrangements can be complicated. Get expert legal and tax advice before entering into one of these arrangements.

4. Preplan and prepay your funeral

Preplanning and prepaying your funeral does not necessarily save you money, but it does remove a key expense that your family or estate must cover upon your death. When you prepay, the money goes into a trust account or insurance fund until your funeral.

You gain certainty over costs because you choose the type of funeral you want in advance. And your family is saved the difficult job of making decisions during a time of grief.

5. Buy permanent life insurance

Life insurance proceeds can be paid to your estate to cover estate costs or left directly to a beneficiary to provide additional amounts to a particular person. The proceeds are always paid tax-free.

Consider a permanent insurance policy for estate planning purposes. Permanent insurance covers you for life, no matter how long you might live. Term insurance does not.

Probate Fees and Life Insurance

When you name a beneficiary for your insurance proceeds, the money is paid directly to your beneficiary. It does not form part of your estate and is not subject to probate fees.

You can also use insurance to cover estate costs. To do this, name your estate as the beneficiary. Your estate will pay probate fees on the insurance proceeds, but it gives your estate the cash to pay debts, taxes, or other obligations. This can avoid the sale of estate assets—such as a home or cottage—that beneficiaries may want to keep in the family. **This is a way to pass on wealth without the burden of tax.**

Cooperation as the Owner of an Insurance Policy

A company is purchasing a universal life policy through a holding on the existence of the proprietor, and funding it over time. The policy is owned by the corporation, which is the beneficiary should the owner die. Excess cash inside the holding company could fund the policy and grow tax-free inside it. "At death, it can be paid on top of the death benefit of the policy into the capital dividend account of the corporation, and paid out on a tax-free basis, minus the adjusted cost base of the policy, to heirs of the owner."

Corporately owned insurance can come with complications. "The proceeds would be open to the claims of the creditors of the company, so that needs to be taken into account."

Insurance as an Insured Annuity

This is useful for retirees who require regular monthly income but want something more tax-efficient than safe but low-interest paying non-registered GICs, or bonds, which are taxed like regular income.

"What we do is we combine an annuity with a life insurance policy." This means there is money available as long as the individual is living, in the form of an annuity, and yet beneficiaries receive funds after the person's death.

Insurance as a Legacy

This is a wealth planning tool for baby boomer generation clients who find that they have more income than needed and are looking to pass it on to the next generation.

"He has used insurance to do that for himself, though in a somewhat unusual way, through a permanent life insurance policy for his infant daughter. He estimates that the plan will cost him less than $60,000 in premiums over a 20-year span to provide her with $750,000 of guaranteed insurance."

"Effectively, what I am doing is giving her a bit of her insurance now," he explained. "By the time she is 25 or 30 and plans to start a family, she does not have this expense every year because she already has her insurance. At the same time, I'm ensuring that I am leaving a legacy for her."

Finally:

One drawback to using insurance as a wealth or estate building strategy is that insurance premiums are not tax deductible in Canada. They are tax-deductible in the United States, but insurance benefits are taxed in the U.S., unlike in Canada. "I would rather not deduct my premiums and have a tax-free lump sum benefit." As an eye opener, first of all, 38% of high-net worth families (those with $1 million or more of investable assets) have not completed any formal estate plan. 57% of people do not have a will . To take full advantage of your hard earned money/assets, put everything in its right place.

Visit www.insurecanadian.com for more information.

Closing Remarks

"Unless you are immortal, you need Life insurance!"

There is a price tag on everything in this world, but the most valuable things, like peace, love and respect, are priceless—they are so precious!

While life is totally unpredictable, we need to plan and invest for peace.We have no control how life treats us; we cannot predict everything, but we can plan for something—to have financial peace, which is linked to our emotional peace—and we are all looking for peace in this world.

My motivation to compile all my ideas in the form of a book was to educate in a very easy and efficient way, and to help families avoid the pain and hassle of not having proper financial planning. TIME is the most important factor in financial planning; but when are in your 20s, you don't think about death, disability, or retirement, while this is the time, if you start saving and establish at least some income replacement, protection will be very affordable and lifelong. This is a very basic book for those who are not ready to start up due to lack of knowledge and fears, that of which consequences are huge.

There are different levels of a financial pyramid but, as I have told, my purpose is to persuade you to at least start doing some very basic planning...Starting up is to have insurance and savings.

Insurance will protect you from the day your coverage is effective, but savings accumulate over time. Both are very important. We have to understand the value and our life stage. Understand your affordability, and plan accordingly.

I have pinpointed the problem and the need, and didn't leave you isolated or wondering what the next step is, and how to do it right.

This book explains about life and living benefits—why to choose; when to choose; and how to choose—along with understanding your life stage. You cannot go wrong with the plan you choose if you have read this book. Chapter 3 will help you understand the need, while the 4th and 5th chapter explains what and how to choose; the 6th chapter will help you understand must-have plan protections.

I also put the effort in chapter 8 to overcome the common myths about insurance by dealing with common objections.

There are scams ,bad products, and inexperienced insurance agents but, once you understand the steps and purchase cycle, you cannot go wrong. Chapter 9 deals with this in detail.

Two facts stand out when it comes to insurance: Canadians rarely think about it, and there's a good chance they do not have enough of it.

Polls and industry statistics consistently find a significant percentage of us do not have enough basic life insurance to support loved ones in the event of an unexpected calamity.

Canadians also seem to ignore the fact that insurance can be a wealth-management and estate-planning tool.

Using insurance to pile up wealth or pass it on to the next generation works best for those who are already in great shape financially: people who have excess money to invest after maximizing their tax shelters such as registered retirement savings plans, tax-free savings accounts, and registered education savings plans.

[74]The only thing you can know about unexpected expenses is that they're coming—for everyone. But having an emergency fund may help alleviate the stress and worry associated with a financial crisis. If your emergency savings are not where they should be, consider taking steps today to create a cushion for the future.

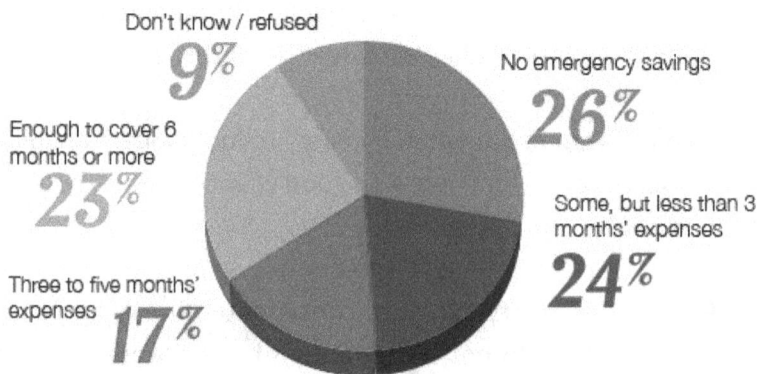

Don't know / refused
9%

No emergency savings
26%

Enough to cover 6 months or more
23%

Some, but less than 3 months' expenses
24%

Three to five months' expenses **17%**

The purpose of this book is to spread awareness about financial planning and to make the readers understand how important it is for a peaceful life. Time is the most important factor; you can't go back in time.

Financial stress is one of biggest stresses in today's world .We spend, on average, about 2 to 3 hours stressing about our finances and debts daily. The solution is to plan education, retirement, and unknown factors, ahead of time.

First, protect and save, and then comes investing. Your needs and priorities get changed at different stages of your life. You have to align with them when it comes to insurance, savings, and investments.

For the scope of this book, only life and living insurance has been discussed, as this is the base—when you are protected, then you can take the next steps.

You always need a qualified advisor to make you understand what you need and how it can be met within the given limitations. There are a few things to know about every life and living product, and you should consider these before buying. Do your homework before blindly trusting your advisor. Make sure your advisor meets the criteria mentioned in chapter 8. Living benefits are equally as important as, and even sometimes more important than, life insurance, as consequences are huge if you are disabled, making no money, and are having someone take care of you—not to mention getting financial stress by looking at bills and fixed expenses piling up.

- 48% of home foreclosures are due to disability
- 2% are due to death
- 90% of disabilities are due to sickness, the major reason for disability
- 10% are due to accidents

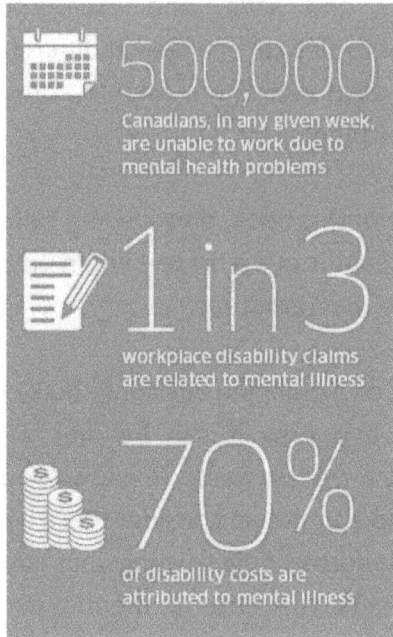

500,000
Canadians, in any given week, are unable to work due to mental health problems

1 in 3
workplace disability claims are related to mental illness

70%
of disability costs are attributed to mental illness

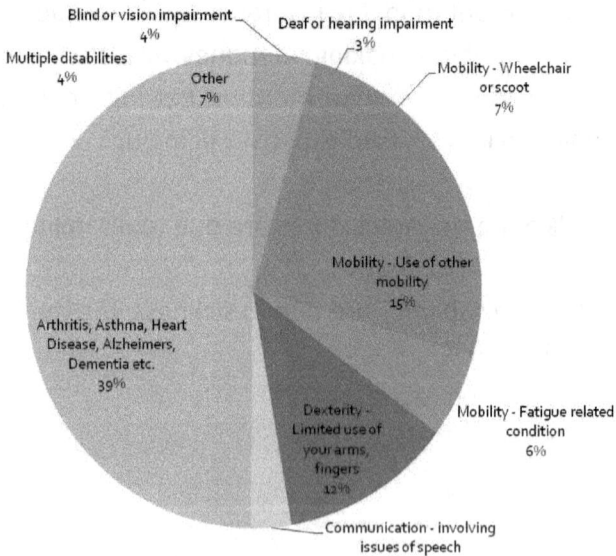

Blind or vision impairment
4%

Deaf or hearing impairment
3%

Multiple disabilities
4%

Other
7%

Mobility - Wheelchair or scoot
7%

Mobility - Use of other mobility
15%

Arthritis, Asthma, Heart Disease, Alzheimers, Dementia etc.
39%

Mobility - Fatigue related condition
6%

Dexterity - Limited use of your arms, fingers
12%

Communication - involving issues of speech

While we are young, we are physically more active; chances of short term disability are higher than in old age.

Here are some mind-blowing numbers:

- [75]Chances of your house burning down: 0.08%
- Chances of being involved in an auto accident: 4%
- Chances of developing a critical illness before you are 65: 35%
- Chances of developing a critical illness before you are 81: 65–70%

Also, it's *very important* to understand what we are covered for under OHIP, EI, CPP, WSIB, Auto Insurance, and Group Employee Benefit Plans.

On the other hand, critical illness protection pays you a one-time lump sum benefit, if you suffer from listed illnesses. A major reason for critical illness is Cancer.

> **Critical Illness Facts:**
>
> - 82% of victims survive their first heart attack
> - 1 in 4 Canadians will develop some form of heart disease during their life-time
> - 1 person in 3 will develop cancer during their lifetime
> - 1 woman in 9 will develop breast cancer during her lifetime
> - 75% of victims survive their first stroke
> - 50,000 Canadians suffer a stroke each year
>
> Source: the Heart & Stroke Foundation of Canada, the Canadian Cancer Society

[76]According to a nationwide study conducted , although 57% of respondents own life insurance, only 28% feel extremely confident in their understanding of life insurance, and 66% don't have a good understanding of how to collect a life insurance payout. Do you fall into this confused category? If so, it's crucial to educate yourself about life insurance, especially if you have people who depend on you (like kids), or have a mortgage or significant amount of debt.

[77]Life insurance gives you the ability to transfer a policy's death benefit, income-tax-free, to beneficiaries. No matter how big the death benefit is—$50,000 or $50 million—your beneficiaries won't pay a single cent of income tax on the money they get. What other investment does that?

It can let you pay for a child's future college education, provide a retirement fund for your spouse, or simply make sure your survivors have the money to live the lifestyle you want for them. People with no life insurance (and even those who do have it) overestimate its cost by three times.

One more important aspect of having a permanent life insurance policy: you can use it as a retirement planning tool as well.

42%

of Americans who own life insurance would consider using it to supplement their retirement income.[1]

Source: LIMRA, 2014 Insurance Barometer Study (survey of American consumers).

Saving vs investing

Living benefits are to make sure you will recover fast without financial worries, and you will not compromise your self respect at your poorest time

You don't need to borrow money or sell your assets. It's an act of love and respect for you and your family . In this book, I've tried to explain the myths about insurance and uncover the reality, especially when we talk about the top reason for not getting insured—that being the assumption that "it's too expensive."

Its very critical to hire an insurance consultant who deals with multiple companies and is efficient enough to design a plan, having life and living benefits together, keeping in mind your budget and needs.

On the other hand, never forget to have an emergency fund that equals your salary of 3 to 6 months; small savings monthly matter a lot

Small steps towards your longterm financial freedom will save you from financial disaster.

Insurance can be a very helpful tool, even in estate planning by avoiding   probate fees, and as a tax efficient strategy. Live today fully, but don't forget to plan for your tomorrow. So, there is a price for everything in this world. Are you ready to pay the price for financial peace? Pay this price, and live respectfully—no   matter   what   life   throws   at   you. You can't plan for everything, but you can for some things. Visit www.insurecanadian.com for more information.

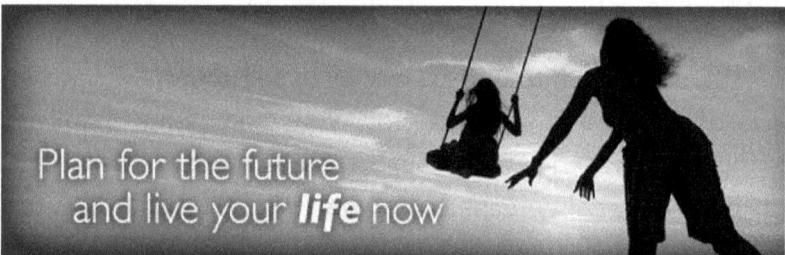

Plan for the future
and live your *life* now

Success and Failure Stories of Families

> *"A man who dies without adequate life insurance should come back and see the mess he has created."*

1. I Wish I'd gotten life insurance *before* I got pregnant

[78]I knew that having our first child meant that getting life insurance should be a top priority for both me and my husband. We researched policies, got a quote for an affordable term life insurance policy, and had our medical exams. Imagine my surprise when, a few weeks later, the agent called me back and told me my new "adjusted" rate.

The cost of my policy had gone from a reasonable monthly fee they'd quoted me, to nearly four times that amount. The reason, he said, was that my cholesterol levels were high. I called my doctor in a panic. "Cholesterol levels always spike during pregnancy," she reassured me, "and they probably won't be back to normal until a few months after you give birth."

After doing some research, I found that it's nearly always better to get a life insurance policy before you get pregnant to avoid potential price hikes brought on by temporary conditions during pregnancy. While some companies will account for the fact that you gained weight due to the pregnancy, factors like higher blood pressure or postpartum depression can also affect your ability to get the best rates.

Now, my daughter is three months old, and I'm still waiting for my numbers to dip before starting again. I really wish I'd known to start this process when trying to conceive instead.

Pay your policies on time

Here's another fact for you: when the worst happens, there is no such thing as a grace period. My mother's homeowner's insurance sent a 2nd notice bill for her policy three days before her house burned down (with her in it) and, when we tried to make the payment five days after that (but before the stated due date), they refused to accept it. We are fighting them, but it's extremely unpleasant to say the least.

Moral of the story: pay your policies on time, and make sure your parents pay theirs.

My husband is dead!

Tim was such a wonderful father and friend. He got up so early every morning and commuted so far to give his family a great life. He was so compassionate and would help anyone. We will miss him dearly, but we know he is in heaven looking down on us.

Tim and I sat down two years ago with a life insurance agent, and they clearly educated us on life insurance and the different types of policies available. They did a thorough needs analysis and then made some recommendations. There was one eye-opener that I remember to this day! Tim was making about $250,000 a year and had two times his salary in life insurance provided by his employer. Sounds Great! Wrong! Our life insurance agent explained that his insurance at work should only be considered as icing on the cake and to manage our life insurance policies outside work. The reason was, if he was laid off, his insurance would cease in most cases. Not to mention he would be much older, or he could have developed a condition that would make him uninsurable. GET THE POINT?

This was the grace in saving my family today. It turns out Tim was laid off from his company and was driving into Chicago for an interview when he was killed in a fatal, multi-car accident. Without the knowledge and insight of the life insurance agent, what we thought was adequate coverage would have left my family and I homeless, considering Tim lost his life insurance benefits when he was laid off.

There aren't many nights that go by that I do not thank God for bringing the life insurance agent into our lives. It's almost two years later, and we are still getting over the death, but the three of us have enough money to handle any challenge that comes our way.

Terri O., Chicago

My Suggestion To Those Reading This:

I would recommend that you take the time to really understand your family's risk exposures if the bread winner was gone. Get a real life insurance agent and have them sit down with you and figure out the right type of policy to cover your family's exposures. As you can see from my case, if we would have not known that Tim's life insurance may have ceased on his termination, I would be homeless today. I am sure there are so many other situations out there. It is the life specialist that will be able to look at your family and expose the holes and needs.

Divorce is hard enough!

When I was divorced, ten years ago, I never really understood the reason why the judge, and my life insurance salesperson, recommended that I get a life insurance policy on my ex-husband, and that I should be the owner.

Now, today, it is all too clear! First of all, knowing my ex-husband, if I was the beneficiary and he was the owner of the policy, I would get nothing. That is because if he stopped paying the premium, I would never have been notified, and my kids and I would have been at risk of getting nothing when the policy expired for nonpayment.

Now, since I am the owner of the policy, I am responsible for the payment of the policy, even though he was required by the judge to make the payments. And you know what? About four years ago, he did stop paying the life premium. I was notified of nonpayment and had the chance to immediately make the payments to bring the policy current. Thank God, I did. He died three months from that day. My family and I now have all the child support we need and a bright future. I am sharing this story because someone did a good deed for me, and I want to pass it on.

My Suggestion To Those Reading This:

Time is moving so fast, and life comes and goes daily. Whether you are getting divorced or are happily married, life insurance is a necessity! Not to mention, it is so cheap. I would highly recommend using life insurance quotes and having a Life Specialist at your service, as I am using them, myself, to review my current policies. Just look at the wealth of real life experiences they are making available. They are genuine and really do care.

You're never too young for life insurance!

Some of your stories brought back so many painful memories; I felt it important to share how one day I insured all my kids and never asked the price.

Back in 1979, Mark, the son of a very close friend of mine, was put to rest. Mark was only 14 years old when he was taken from us.

For the first 8 years of Mark's life, he was as healthy and normal as any 8 year old kid. At the age of 9, Mark started having bad stomach cramps and started losing lots of weight. After many months of tests and hospitalizations, Mark was diagnosed as having Crohns disease. It took 4 years, three major surgeries, lots of horrible health food, and a colostomy to finally get Mark's life back on track.

Everything was going great for Mark; that was until a year later, at the age of 14, when Mark started having sores and other immune issues. It turns out that he had received the HIV virus from a blood transfusion during one of his surgeries. Unfortunately, Mark died within the year.

Now, you can imagine the funeral costs, the doctor bills from the original surgeries, and now the HIV related costs that followed. Our friends did have medical insurance through work, but let me just say, their lifetime cap was reached quickly. The unfortunate part was they had plenty of insurance on the parents, but none on the kids.

Kim K., Ontario

My Suggestion To Those Reading This:

If you have kids, get them covered while they are young; you never know. For us, thank God, we never had to use any of our policies. Instead, the cash values in the accounts have accumulated to nice little nest eggs for our children.

Thank God we never needed it. Now we have money for retirement!

Thirty two years later, and I am as ornery as the day I married Linda. Linda and I were on the internet looking for information on annuities and came across your site. I read your stories and wanted to tell ours.

I bought a permanent policy, 32 years ago, because I loved my wife and, if I died, I wanted to ensure she and my family could continue having the same level of living. Now, if I didn't die, we would have enough money for retirement. HA! HA! HA! I beat the odds and outlived the need for life insurance as my family has all grown up and moved away. I get the cash! I am sure I will die some day but, until then, I do know I have enough money for Linda and I to last a lifetime.

Ted H., Toronto

My Suggestion To Those Reading This:

Read all these stories until you are convinced you need life insurance. Face the facts: DEATH is the only guarantee in life. You brought your family into the world, and it is your responsibility to protect them. Use their life insurance calculator and find how much you need for your family, and then get a quote. It's FREE. You win no matter what! If you die, your family gets the cash, tax free; and, if you outlive the need, you can get the cash and be like Linda and I.

If you still are not convinced, just start asking people around you if they know anyone that died without having life insurance, and what happened.

Tom, You Really Hurt Us!

To My Dead Husband, Tom,

Why were you so against insurance? You always chuckled and laughed that you would never die, and I would just remarry. Well, guess what? You died, one year later! It's now two years later; all our money is gone, and I have some real physical and mental challenges.

I am left with our daughter Susan, with NO HOME, and am working two jobs; and I have bills coming out my $##, and the damn collectors will not stop calling. They are even calling our friends and my work. The doctor bills for your heart attack alone were in excess of $90,000.

The fun and laughter is now gone, and we are really hurting! When I really think about it, I believe I am as much to blame as you are. I should have opened my mind and imagined the alternative picture the life guy was painting. Instead, I chose to laugh about it and assumed it would never happen to us.

The joke is on me! I am not remarried and most likely will not get married ever again. When someone dies, it is amazing the sorrow and pain that comes to the surface.

I want to let you know that I now have a policy on myself, and I make sure it is the first bill paid. If something ever happens to me, I want Susan to be protected. You know what kills me the most? For only $30 month, we could have been protected.

Tina

Daddy, Thanks for Caring...

I remember it like it was yesterday. It was December 14, 2001, at 3am in the morning, and my mom was screaming. I ran in the room; my mom was screaming that dad had a heart attack.

You expect people these days to have a heart attack after they are 50 or 60 years old. In my case, my dad died when he was 33 years old.

I do not think you can ever be prepared for what will happen in the future. My dad never got to see his insurance money, but it sure helped us pay for the funeral and the doctor bills, and enabled us to keep our home and provide for the many challenges yet to come.

Thank You Daddy; I love you.

P.S. I will graduate high school this year and go on to college at the University of Nebraska.

My Suggestion To Those Reading This:

Parents, you brought your kids into the world. Plan ahead, and protect them.

Title Experience: **He said no, but I said YES!**

Dear Tammy,

We miss you so much, but I want to let you know that I appreciate you so much, and am thankful for having listened to the life insurance specialist three years ago, even though I was so against insurance.

I know you are no longer with us and how wonderful it must be in heaven. I just wanted to let you know that we are all ok. The kids are all growing quickly and our new nanny is wonderful. At first, I was worried how I was going to be able to continue working and take care of a family at the same time. Although we all miss you every minute of the day, your planning and forethought has sure made it easier, not having to worry about who will take care of the kids and the house. Instead, we get to focus on you and our memories.

Tammy, thanks for being so persistent and forceful.

Your husband, Ted

If you are reading this, and trying to decide whether you need life insurance, ask yourself this question: "What will happen to my family and friends if I die?" and "Are they worth the $25 a month?"

Finally,

I hope these experiences and scenarios were helpful in understanding why life insurance is so important. Many people ask us, "Well, great, now what?" Follow the steps explained in Chapter #9—your family is worth it!

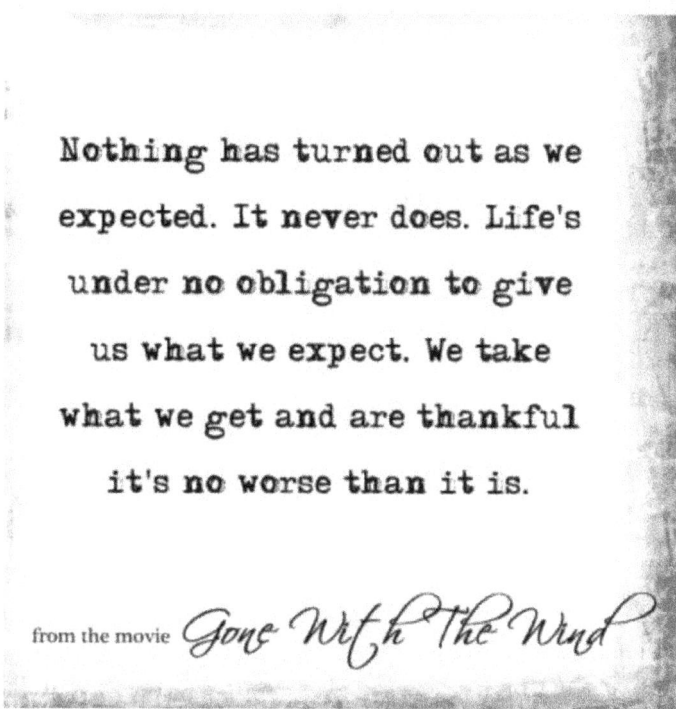

> Nothing has turned out as we expected. It never does. Life's under no obligation to give us what we expect. We take what we get and are thankful it's no worse than it is.
>
> from the movie *Gone With The Wind*

[69] www.theglobeandmail.com
[70] www.rbcds.com
[71] www.firstinsurance.info
[72] mycoverage.ca
[73] www.theglobeandmail.com
[74] www.weeklypostnc.com
[75] www.insureye.com
[76] www.quoteguardian-blog.com
[77] www.firstinsurance.info
[78] www.forbes.com/sites/learnvest/2013/07/15/i-sure-could-have-used-life-insurance-3-true-stories

References

www.insurecanadian.com
Cic.gc.ca
http://www.forbes.com
http://www.investopedia.com
http://business.financialpost.com
http://www.torontosun.com
Serviceontario.ca
https://www.sunlife.ca
http://www.assante.com
https://retirehappy.ca
http://www.financialplanninginfoguide.com
https://www.thebalance.com
https://www.lifehappens.org
http://www.bankrate.com
http://www.limra.com
https://www.northamericancompany.com
http://dreamprotector.com
picturesquote.com
What's Wrong with Your Life Insurance by Norman Dacey
Risk Your Business, Risk Your Life by Tony Bourke

www.ingramcontent.com/pod-product-compliance
Lightning Source LLC
Chambersburg PA
CBHW030841210326
41521CB00025B/557